Managed
by Morons

Managed
by Morons

The Path to a Thriving Organisation

Avoiding the Pitfalls That Stand in Your Way

James Lawther

Squawk **POINT**
Nottingham

Squawk Point

95 Cyprus Road

Nottingham

NG3 5ED

United Kingdom

e-Mail: james.lawther@squawkpoint.com

Website: https://squawkpoint.com

First published in Great Britain in 2023.

© 2023 James Lawther.

ISBN 978-1-7394389-0-6

Cover Design: The New Fat, https://www.thenewfat.co.uk/

Editing and Proofreading: Jakki Bendell, https://jakkibendell.co.uk/

010823-PB-KDP

Published in Nottinghamshire

Dedication

To the fed-up and frustrated middle manager.

I have felt your pain.

Thanks to:

Jimmy, for keeping me honest.
Bernie, for egging me on.
Hazel, for pointing out the obvious.
Jon and Mark, for proving it can be done.
Andy and Dave, for their harsh but fair critiques.
Jakki, for her consistency.
Hayleigh, for paint and pictures.
Christine, for her tolerance.

And the Morons, for their unending inspiration.

All of our social problems arise out of doing the wrong thing righter. The more efficient you are at doing the wrong thing, the wronger you become. It is much better to do the right thing wronger than the wrong thing righter!

If you do the right thing wrong and correct it, you get better!

~Russel L. Ackoff

Contents

Figures

Introduction

In the late 1980s, I was a bright young thing. I had landed a place on one of the world's most prestigious graduate trainee programmes, and I thought I would be the youngest chief executive of a FTSE 100 company ever. Things didn't go to plan.

Twenty-five years later, I was stranded at East Croydon railway station. It was well past 9pm on a cold, wet, miserable Tuesday in January. My wife and daughters (and mortgage) were hundreds of miles distant, my career hadn't so much plateaued as nose-dived, and my boss was a bully and an idiot (a potent if somewhat unwelcome combination). The evening's delights consisted of a pizza for one and the hotel minibar. The only thing I had to look forward to was a four-day Easter holiday, which was a long time away.

I wanted to enjoy my career. I still had 20 years to go, but success no longer looked like becoming a captain of industry. I had no desire to be scheduled into meetings until 7pm every Friday. Besides, the commuters sitting in First Class look even more suicidal than the rest of us. Success wasn't about being a "yes man" and selling my soul to the corporation. It had much more to do with my bit of the organisation thriving and my team taking pleasure in challenging and rewarding work. Yet at every turn, something or (more often) somebody got in the way.

I realised that most corporate ills are self-inflicted. It isn't competitors, suppliers or customers that cause the problems, but other parts of the business. Most management boards and leadership teams act like the court of King Henry VIII. There is as much political infighting, back-stabbing and rivalry, with a similar amount of progress.

Corporations are competitive places, and that competition plays out in two distinct ways.

The first competition is between organisations for market share or funding. Businesses provide products or services, and the best-run organisation wins. Starbucks wins at coffee, Google wins at search, and Harvard wins at management education. Of course, people will debate who is the top dog (if you are in the Midlands, I will vouch that my local coffee shop, 200°, sells the best Americano), but you understand my point. However, winning isn't a foregone conclusion. Kodak won at photography and Nokia won at mobile phones, but arguably, Apple now wins at both those games.

The second competition is within organisations for status and power. Individuals strive to outdo each other as they climb the corporate ladder. This type of competition is linked to the first. The more competent somebody is at running an organisation, the higher they should rise. But as anybody who has ever laughed at a Dilbert cartoon will know, seniority and capability don't always go hand in hand.[1]

The problem is that success in the second competition (to build a career) can often lead to defeat in the first. Nobody wants to work for a failing organisation, yet sometimes the rush to clamber up the slippery pole gets in the way.

> *There is more conflict within corporations than between them, and it is generally less ethical.*
>
> *~ Peter Drucker*

I decided to worry less about the corporate ladder and more about my department. I wanted to win the external game and build a thriving organisation. Only some people will rise through the ranks to become chief executives, but every manager can make their business jump with activity and enthusiasm. I wanted more good days, with happy customers and employees, and to take a little personal satisfaction in building a slick operation.

This book shows what I discovered. It will explain how to make your team, office, branch, business or corporation excel. (Though, for God's sake, don't claim to be "world-class". Nobody will believe you, and we will all snigger at your arrogance).

The book isn't packed full of tools, techniques, models or diagrams. Plenty of material out there is better at laying out approaches and methods. Instead of telling you what to do, it will explain why to do it. I promise it will achieve four things:

1. Explain why many organisations are so mediocre.
2. Challenge what you have been taught about management.
3. Show you what to do differently.
4. Entertain you.

When you have finished reading, I hope you make your business sing. I want you and your staff to make your organisation so good that customers will beg you for more. Then I'd like you to bask in the reflected glory. In short, I want you to thrive. You never know; somebody might even thank you for a job done well.

Incidentally, if you have never been to East Croydon railway station, don't bother. It has nothing to recommend it.

Part 1.

Building Capability

Chapter 1:
Dysfunctional Organisations

Dictators, District Services and Shared Management Patterns

Before eulogising about thriving, productive businesses, let's explore how it feels to work in a failing one by telling the story of an organisation that made hideous mistakes. At best, this should provide insight into what can go wrong. At the very least, it will make you realise that where you work isn't so bad after all.

China's Great Leap Forward

From 1958 to 1962, Mao Zedong, chairman of the Communist Party of China, attempted to transform his country. He wanted to change it from an agricultural economy into an industrial powerhouse, a country that would rival Britain and the United States. Mao's desire to overtake Britain within 15 years became "the guiding ideology of the party and the country."[2]

Chairman Mao forced through many radical changes to achieve his dream. He abolished private ownership of land and property, creating state-operated communes instead. The Communist Party then set these communes stringent food production targets to feed the cities and provide goods for export. New agricultural methods were adopted. The government enforced close planting of seeds to improve yields. Manure was concentrated on the most fertile land to increase productivity, whilst other land was left fallow. The "Four Pests" campaign was introduced to eradicate mosquitos, rats, flies and sparrows, and the government declared that "Birds are public animals of capitalism."[3]

As well as improving agricultural output, the communes were urged to build backyard steel furnaces to boost industrial output. Loudspeakers boomed out propaganda and songs to motivate the people and encourage compliance with the new policies.[4] Everywhere, local party officials swung into action to force through the changes.

The peasants and workers battled to build and operate the backyard furnaces. They stripped local forests of trees to fire the forges. Knives, pots, pans and other "scrap materials" were requisitioned and then melted to produce low-quality pig iron. The struggle to hit production targets took people away from work in the fields.

Of the four pests, sparrows were the easiest to attack. Workers banged pots and pans together incessantly. The resulting racket frightened the birds so much they wouldn't land in the trees. Many died from the exhaustion of endless flying. People sought out sparrows' nests, smashed their eggs and killed their chicks. The party spread propaganda to urge the activity on, especially in rural areas.

"Killing sparrows serves to protect crops. Sparrows in cities and forest areas do not necessarily have to be eliminated."[5]

The Soviet agronomist Trofim Lysenko was the man behind many of these agricultural innovations, and he had the ear of Chairman Mao.[6] Unfortunately, his beliefs were misguided. Close planting of seedlings didn't increase yields; it reduced them as the plants competed for resources. The densely planted seedlings also made farm labour difficult, as workers couldn't move easily between the plants. Yet the authorities didn't listen to the objections. On hearing the farmers' complaints, Liu Shaoqi, Mao's deputy, suggested that peasants use tweezers to weed the seedlings.

Despite the havoc caused by Lysenko's ideas, the weather in 1958 was perfect for agriculture, and it should have been a bumper harvest. But because farmers were so busy with Mao's steel furnaces and other diktats, much of the crop rotted in the fields. A plague of locusts exacerbated the problem as the insect population flourished without its usual predators, the rodents and sparrows that the peasants had scared off.[7] The harvest that year was disastrous, but few dared to admit it.

Local officials, motivated by fear or power, declared record-breaking yields. Senior bureaucrats then swooped in to commandeer the grain "surplus". It was taken to fill government warehouses, leaving nothing for the farmers to eat, and the lack of food resulted in widespread famine in rural areas.

As disquiet spread amongst the population, there were vicious attacks on anybody who challenged or questioned the policies. When the head of one agricultural commune dared to point out the obvious, that there wasn't any food, a party leader warned him, "That's right-deviationist thinking. You're viewing the problem in an overly simplistic matter."

Local leaders started covering up the famine and blaming the peasants to protect their positions. When Mao visited Henan province in 1958, the fields he saw were carefully prepared. Regional administrators had dug up healthy seedlings from other areas and transplanted them, creating lush, densely packed fields where Mao travelled, so all he saw was abundance.

Only one of Mao's senior leaders, Marshal Peng Dehuai, the minister of defence, spoke out about what was happening. Mao denounced him as bourgeois and sacked him. His successor Lin

Biao then purged the military of Dehuai's supporters. Mao cowed his opposition. Gangs of his political supporters harassed or killed anybody who dared speak out. The censorship became so severe that doctors were even forbidden from using the word "starvation" on death certificates.

Despite the famine, China was a net grain exporter between 1958 and 1960. When news of the disaster reached the outside world, the Japanese secretly offered to ship 100,000 tonnes of wheat to China. The Chinese refused the offer. When asked about the famine in a news conference in 1961, John F. Kennedy said, "We've had no indication from the Chinese Communists that they would welcome any offer of food."

Chairman Mao did not want to lose face and admit failure. Estimates vary on how many people starved to death. The most that has ever been formally admitted is 22 million, though some estimate the number was as high as 55 million.[8] But those are just big numbers; it is the small stories that illustrate China's plight.[9]

One man was found guilty of stealing a sweet potato, so officials forced him to eat excrement, whilst another was forced to bury his son alive for stealing a handful of grain. Another horror story is the tale of a teenage orphan who killed and ate her four-year-old brother. In a different village, 44 of the 45 residents died.

In an internal Party communiqué in 1959, Mao admitted that, "Much of the falsehood has been prompted by the upper levels through boasting, pressure and reward, leaving little alternative to those below."

Two years later, in 1961, the dictatorship curtailed the agricultural policies, and food production rose. China stopped exporting grain and accepted shipments from Canada and Australia. All the country's leadership had to do was face the issues and admit their failings. Arrogance, self-deception and fear got in the way. Mao's China was a hideously dysfunctional organisation.

The Media Relations Department

Fortunately, not every organisation is as large and powerful as Chairman Mao's, but on a smaller level, similar behaviour occurs. A few years ago, I posted this article online:[10]

Distorting the System

The UK Government instigated a national target to improve the ambulance service's performance. It stipulated that 75% of life-threatening emergencies should have an ambulance on the scene within eight minutes of the call.

The East of England Ambulance Service invested in "Rapid Response Vehicles" (RRVs) to hit the target. These are medically equipped cars and motorcycles. They are less expensive than full-blown ambulances and don't need to be staffed by two paramedics. Consequently, they provide cheap capacity. This is very helpful if you are trying to respond to emergencies within eight minutes.

Having a paramedic on the scene quickly is a good thing. But it is difficult to transport an 80-year-old man having a heart attack to a hospital on the back of a motorbike. A system that takes medical care to patients differs from one that takes patients to medical care.

One senior paramedic claimed, "The trust has become so fixated with hitting the target by sending out RRVs to 'stop the clock'. Care, patient safety and dignity are being badly compromised."

I based the post on an article in the national press.[11] I was making a point about the effect of targets on organisational design.

Applying political and managerial pressure to hit targets rarely improves productivity or performance.

A couple of days after posting the piece, I received an angry e-mail from the media relations department of the East of England Ambulance Service. It informed me in no uncertain terms that:

- The ambulance service exists to save lives, not to provide a taxi service to the hospital.
- The East of England Ambulance Service does not have motorcycles.
- They wouldn't put an 80-year-old man on the back of a motorcycle (even if they had one).
- I needed to update my blog post.
- If I didn't, they would report me to the Independent Press Standards Organisation and take me to court under the Defamation Act 2013.
- In future, I should ask before publishing.

I hadn't intended to denigrate the work carried out by the East of England (or any other) Ambulance Service, so I offered to publish a follow-on post. It became apparent that the East of England Ambulance Service media relations department did not want their comments made public. They were only interested in removing adverse publicity.

What was it like to work for that organisation at the time? All I know for sure is that the management team thought it was a better use of public money to hire a media relations department to harass second-rate bloggers rather than to invest it in medical staff.

On a positive note, the experience taught me to be more careful with my fact-checking. I can categorically tell you that the East of England Ambulance Service hasn't yet invested in motorcycles. Their media relations department did, however, neglect to point out that they use bicycles instead.[12] *

A Management Pattern

The pattern that links dysfunctional organisations, be they dictatorships or local public services, is how their managers behave and the culture they create. Culture is nebulous. There is more to it than "the way we do things around here." Behaviour is only the tip of the iceberg; many thoughts and beliefs underpin it. But the tip of the iceberg is revealing. There are plenty of hints when things are rotten.

Destructive Behaviours

- Managers obsess about command-and-control.
- Targets are rife.
- Intimidation and casting blame are core competencies.
- Leaders don't listen.
- Staff don't speak up (or feel they can't).
- Failures are buried.
- Good news abounds.
- Perception (be that propaganda or media relations) is more important than performance.

You will recognise these behaviours if you have worked in a large bureaucratic organisation (why else would you be reading this book?) Not all organisations are the same, some tackle their challenges differently, but the secret to a thriving organisation is culture. People's behaviour impacts performance far more than any technology, management idea or whiz-bang initiative ever will.

---

* That was petty of me. I spend a lot of time in Norwich and if I ever have need of a paramedic, I will be very grateful if one turns up on a bicycle. If I need an ambulance, I'd be grateful for one of those as well.

Summary

Key Points

- The antithesis of a productive organisation is a dysfunctional one.
- Dysfunctional organisations come in all shapes and sizes.
- A repeating management or behavioural pattern occurs within dysfunctional organisations.
- An organisation that doesn't break this pattern will never truly thrive.

Actions

- Re-read the list of destructive management behaviours.
- List any that are present in your organisation.

> *Culture eats strategy for breakfast.*
>
> *~ Peter Drucker*

Chapter 2:
The Productivity Lever

The Art of Coping and the People Paradox

It is fine to highlight the importance of culture, but culture alone won't enhance an organisation's output and keep its customers or shareholders happy. Assuming all the behavioural problems have been solved (which is a bit of a leap, but we will return to that problem), where should an organisation focus its improvement efforts? Where is the productivity lever?

The Art of Coping

I ran a back-office operation that collected and processed data a few years ago. Other than the man at the tax office, I suspect we handled more data than anybody else in the country. I was the "Head of Keying In". It wasn't a glamorous job; people would scream like billy-oh if their data wasn't available on time.

My job was simple. I just had to ensure everyone could cope with the never-ending torrent of data and files pushed our way. The more competent we were at dealing with the ever-changing demands that the business made of us, the better the quality of the service we could provide to the organisation. It was a straightforward relationship. If our ability to cope went up, service quality also went up. If we did what we said we would do, when we said we would do it, everybody was happy… Well, at least nobody complained. Which, for us, amounted to happiness.

Unfortunately, there was a complication. People would keep adding new, more complicated tasks to our to-do list. There was either more to do (volume went up), or the tasks changed, and things became more complex (variety went up). These two things added to the overall workload we had to manage. As our workload increased, our ability to cope with it all decreased, and life became more challenging. Then, as you can imagine, the quality of the service we provided fell.

When this happened, there were a couple of simple ways to improve the situation. The first involved our staff. We could hire more people and train them. The bigger and better the team we had, the easier it was to cope with the work and customer service improved.

The second was to develop our systems. By systems, I don't just mean computer systems. I mean processes, machinery, policies and everything that made up the business system we worked with. The slicker our systems were, the less time we wasted. Robust systems reduced workload and hence improved our ability to cope. Unfortunately, both extra staff and new systems cost money. As we were already a big fat cost line in somebody's profit and loss account, laying my hands on investment was tough.

We were one giant machine that sucked up money and threw out a service and in that way we were no different to a hospital, rubbish collection depot, railway or charity. The dynamics were the same. My daily grind was identical to every other manager I have ever met. It was one long juggling act, coping with an increasing workload, demanding customers and insufficient resources.

Now comes the nasty bit. If we reached the point where we couldn't cope, we would invariably mess something up (though we used stronger language to express this). Somebody would forget something as they were busy spinning plates elsewhere. Or a system would choke on its workload and give up the ghost. When that happened, things would quickly whirl away from us in a horrible out-of-control fashion. The more we messed things up, the more work we created for ourselves trying to fix issues. The extra workload made it less likely that we could cope, which meant it was inevitable that we would mess something else up.

Some would call the dynamic a vicious spiral. We had another term, but it isn't printable. It was not a nice place to be. It is why people with jobs like mine tended to come and go. Things could quickly become so bad that we jumped, or maybe we just got pushed.

The system I managed looked a bit like this:

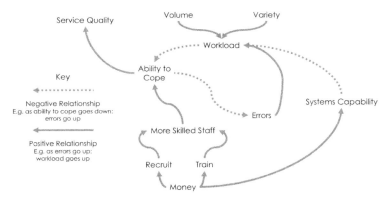

Figure 1: The Ability to Cope

If you are considering applying for a job like the one I had, let me repeat myself so you know exactly what you are letting yourself in for. Sooner or later, your organisation will falter, and you will spiral downward. When this happens, there are only three ways to reduce the pain:

- Hire more people.
- Improve the people.
- Improve the system.

Hiring more people is the easiest, but it costs money your boss won't want to give you (and throwing money at a problem hardly counts as a productivity gain). This leaves you with two options: improve the people or improve the system.

The People Paradox

Almost every large organisation has a human resources (HR) department that helps it develop the capability of its people. Conventional wisdom is that if an organisation improves its people, it will improve its performance. Whilst there is truth in that, it is an opaque truth. A management paradox is at play, which few recognise or understand.

Business performance has little to do with people, yet a business depends entirely on its people's performance.

Like all good paradoxes, it is oxymoronic. It is best explained by telling the story of a quality guru called W. Edwards Deming who plied his trade in the second half of the 20th century. He was big news after the Second World War. Deming was one of the men credited with helping Japan revive its economy after the bombings of Nagasaki and Hiroshima.

Deming used to hold lectures to explain his management philosophy, to which thousands of people flocked. He invariably ran a demonstration in these lectures called "The Red Bead Experiment".

Deming carried a shoebox to these meetings. It was full of white beads, with a smattering of red ones thrown in. He also had a paddle with bead-shaped divots drilled into it so that when it was pushed into the box and pulled back out again, it would carry out a selection of white and red beads.[13]

Deming would then concoct a story about needing some workers to manufacture beads. The manufacturing process involved pushing the paddle into the box and pulling out the beads. White beads were wanted, whereas red beads were defects. Of course, some workers were more "skilled" at producing good quality white beads than others due to natural variation and pure dumb luck.

Deming would run a series of production runs, praising workers for good performance and admonishing those with poor quality. He would set specific, measurable, achievable, realistic, time bound (SMART) targets, offer training and advice, put the low performers on performance plans, give bonus payments to the high performers and generally drag the whole thing out for 20 minutes.* The point of Deming's show was straightforward. In a business as simple as a box full of beads and a wooden paddle, organisational performance had little to do with how people behaved and everything to do with system design. Deming wasted his time "managing" and "motivating" staff, creating goals and incentivising people. He would then point out that he'd have had much more success if he had spent time picking red beads out of the box (building system capability).

Business performance has little to do with people. Our organisations are infinitely more complicated than a box of beads, so we will get infinitely more bang for our buck if we work on improving the system rather than improving the people.

Frank and the Spanner: A Management Fable

In the Midlands, there is a factory. The people who work there make bits that fit into other bits that eventually find their way into washing machines, lawnmowers and radiator valves. It is a grimy old factory that bumps along at the bottom of the Industrial supply chain, just about making enough money to keep its doors open.

---

* My description doesn't do the event justice. It is worth a quick search online to find a video to watch. Search for "Deming red bead experiment".

The owners have tried different initiatives to increase the factory's performance for many years, but none amounted to much. The staff just ignored them. They knew nothing would change (nothing ever really changes in the Midlands), and the plant owners got progressively more and more exasperated. The owners appointed a Bright Young Thing (BYT) as the new plant supervisor to solve their productivity problem. He was fresh out of business school with the shiniest pair of shoes anybody had ever seen.

The BYT was convinced that he knew the solution. Instead of force-feeding the staff another top-down initiative, he would get close to the work, listen to the people and understand their problems. "You can't transform your organisation if you don't know your organisation." Or so he'd been taught.

Off the BYT trotted to the shop floor, where he met Frank. Frank was not a bright young thing. Frank had come into this world a fully paid-up member of the awkward squad. He didn't like anyone telling him what to do, he didn't like managers, he didn't like productivity initiatives, and he certainly didn't like BYTs. "Bend over, here comes another one" thought Frank.

"I'm here to help you improve productivity" said the BYT.

"Really?" muttered Frank

"Yes, tell me what I can do to help."

Frank shrugged. He'd heard it before,

"Nobody ever listens here", replied Frank. "Why should I waste my time telling you what we can do to get better?"

"This time, it will be different. I will listen, I will give you what you need, and we can make this business great together." The BYT liked to lay it on a bit thick.

"OK", said Frank. "Get me a new spanner."

The BYT looked at the spanner Frank had in his hand. It wasn't any old spanner. It was a heavyweight, chrome-

vanadium, open-ended slogging spanner; they cost a pretty penny. The BYT winced. How was he going to justify buying another spanner? But he'd committed to Frank that he would listen, so off he wandered to the factory stores to see what he could do.

"Do you know how much those things cost?" gasped the head storeman. "Is it for Frank? The old git has been angling for one of those for years. He already has a perfect spanner. You can't trust him. If you give him another one, it will only end up on eBay. Tell him he can't have it. Give him one, and everybody else will want one!" So the BYT returned to Frank empty-handed and told him the news.

"Now there is a thing", grunted Frank.

"Here you come, spouting all your engagement claptrap, I must listen to my staff, they know what to do, I must empower them, it will boost morale, blah bleeding blah blah. And what do you do about it when somebody has the guts to ask you for something?"

"What?" replied the BYT

"Bugger all!"

Frank was not a happy man.

The BYT slowly wandered off back to the storeroom. He told the storeman to hand over the spanner.

"You will have to sign for it and get it authorised!"

So, the BYT took the chitty and walked upstairs to see the chairman, who raised his eyebrows and eventually authorised the spanner. Ten minutes later, the BYT was back on the shop floor, spanner in hand. He handed it over to Frank.

Frank took the spanner, somewhat bemused, then, with one spanner in each hand, started to adjust the motor. Would you believe it? The machine began to run faster. Then Frank took his spanners and walked down the production line towards the next piece of equipment.

The moral of the story is a point that many managers find hard to swallow. Our business systems are complicated, and no one person knows how they work, no matter how clever or senior. **A business depends entirely on its people's performance**. The best way to increase the capability of your systems is to engage your employees in the improvement effort. They are the only ones who know how their bit of the system works. If your employees aren't with you, you might as well give up now.

Business performance has little to do with people, yet a business depends entirely on its people's performance.

The way to resolve the paradox is to exploit the difference between in and on. People have minimal effect on performance when they are working **in** the system. However, they are critical when you are working **on** the system. These are not the same thing. Obsessing about creating a perfectly productive employee is futile. Even if it wasn't, they could always leave. Improving the people is a poor strategy (yet engaging them in improving the system is all important).

Capability Counts

If you find yourself in a vicious productivity spiral but like your job (or at least your pay cheque) and want to keep it, there is only one way out.

- ~~Hire more people~~ (expensive).
- ~~Improve the people~~ (ineffective).
- Improve the system.

The solution is to improve the system and build capability. Capability doesn't have to be a multi-million-pound IT investment. A team can do a thousand and one things to make work slicker and simpler. Each one only costs a little time. They include writing a macro or clarifying a work instruction, mending a faulty machine and creating better management information, speeding up a conveyor belt or reordering the work allocation. The list verges on being infinite.

There are always other ways to develop a system, but they will only happen if an organisation takes a little pain and frees up some of its employees' time to complete them. Building capability is tough when caught in a vicious productivity spiral, but it is the only way out. Once an enhancement has been implemented, the organisation can re-invest the time saved in that slight improvement in another and another. That way, a manager can reverse the spiral from vicious to virtuous. Like all good advice, this is easier said than done. But there is only one productivity lever: building system capability.

An organisation must create virtuous productivity spirals to thrive. It will only achieve that if it allows its staff time to work both on the business and in it. The productivity challenge is creating an environment where **everybody has two jobs: doing their job and improving it.** Somewhere one of your competitors is busy writing that macro.

> *It is not necessary to change. Survival is not mandatory.*
>
> *~ W. Edwards Deming*

Summary
Key Points
- There are three ways to improve performance: hire more people, improve the people or improve the system.

- Hiring more people is expensive.
- It is more effective to improve the system than to improve the people.
- A manager's job is to create an environment where the shop floor (and everybody else) is engaged in improving the business's systems.
- People are critical if they are working on the system rather than in it.

Actions

- Review your objectives and project list.
- How much time are you focusing on improving the system?
- How much do you spend managing the people (objective setting, performance reviews, development action plans and all-round people management)?
- Change your work balance to focus more on improving your systems and processes.
- Schedule time to observe what is happening on your shop floor.
- Be respectful and ask your staff what stops them from doing a better job.
- Write down what you learnt.
- Fix something and invest the saved time in fixing something else.

Chapter 3:
How to Pull the Lever

The Performance Pyramid

Understanding where to find the productivity lever is an interesting intellectual exercise, but the knowledge is only helpful if you use it. There are plenty of obstacles and behaviours that will get in the way.

Mark Jenkins is the professor of Business Strategy at Cranfield School of Management. He studied Formula One racing, a viciously competitive industry, to understand how the teams develop as they strive to win. To explain his discoveries, Jenkins created the "Performance Pyramid", a simple yet thought-provoking model.[14] It details the three elements of winning organisations and how they support one another: focus, learning and culture.

Focus

Jenkins believes that great organisations are clear about what is important to them. They have a vivid sense of purpose and know what they are trying to achieve. They know what winning looks like. As organisations grow and expand, they lose this focus, and managers start to fixate on their personal targets and objectives rather than those of the business. Different agendas abound, and organisations lose their way.

Learning

Highly productive organisations constantly adapt and build new capabilities to remain competitive. They can only do this if they learn. They use the "Learning Cycle", or as Jenkins calls it: plan, do and review.

They plan an experiment, do it, check to see what happened and act on the outcomes. They then plan their next experiment and start the cycle again. The critical part of the cycle is review, where teams use quantitative and qualitative data to see what happened and change their approach accordingly. They don't get caught up in analysis paralysis, spending months trying to get more data and developing perfect knowledge. Instead, they strive for constant experimentation, developing an idea, trying it out and learning from it. The faster they cycle through the experimental loop, the quicker they build knowledge. Every time they learn something useful, they bake it into their systems and processes, constantly improving their capabilities.

Culture

Jenkins claims that you can't have a learning organisation if you don't have the right culture. He cites four critical cultural aspects and behaviours that the best organisations show.

- **Constant communication:** Everybody knows what is happening and what needs to happen next. The communication is relevant and face-to-face. An intranet portal or a string of e-mails doesn't work as people ignore them.
- **A no-blame philosophy:** There is psychological safety, and people are honest. The opposite is a culture where managers take their pound of flesh if anything goes wrong. In an environment like that, staff aren't prepared to try anything new for fear of failure. They will also be quick to blame others

when things don't work. Consequently, problems are hidden and never get fixed.

- **A long-term perspective:** If there is constant pressure to change and adapt, it is easy to lose sight of where you are going and become too responsive to external factors. It is hard to steer a steady course if you are constantly buffeted by the here and now. Productive cultures always maintain sight of the long-term goal.
- **A one-team mindset:** In great organisations, people work together, collaborating and coordinating their efforts. Jenkins points out that customers aren't concerned about who does what within an organisation. They only care about the outcome they are paying for. It is all-important that a business acts as one unit rather than a crowd of separate people and departments.

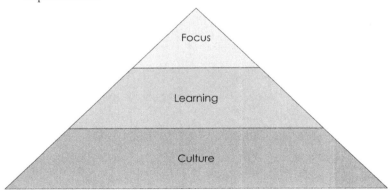

Figure 2: The Performance Pyramid

What Are Managers For?

The team's job is to ensure that the organisation keeps learning and adding new capabilities to the organisation's system. The leader, however, must play a twofold role. They need to create focus and maintain culture. A manager's job isn't micromanaging their staff but creating an environment where people can do their best work. Yet there are so many ways organisations can trip over themselves as they try to excel. From corporate giants to small departments, managers struggle with even the first step, creating focus.

Summary

Key Points

- Thriving organisations are clear about what they want to thrive at.
- Those organisations are continually learning and developing in pursuit of that goal.
- They have a culture that underpins their ability to learn.
- Managers don't micromanage their staff but set the direction and culture that supports them as they build learning and embed capability.

Actions

Assess your organisation:

- Does it have a clear unifying purpose or disparate departmental goals?
- Is it constantly testing, learning and improving, or are most staff concerned with managing the status quo and telling a good story?
- Have managers created an environment and culture that allows, encourages and helps staff to experiment and build organisational capability? Or do managers strive to command-and-control their teams?

Part 2.

Creating Focus

Chapter 4:
What is Your Purpose?

Lessons From Peter Drucker and the Cheshire Cat

When I was in my twenties, I went on a management course. Twenty graduate trainees sat in a conference centre as different presenters shuffled in and out to give us the benefit of their wisdom. I am embarrassed to say that the only one that stayed in my memory reminded me of the story by Lewis Carroll.

Alice's Adventures in Wonderland

"Would you tell me, please, which way I ought to go from here?"

"That depends a good deal on where you want to get to," said the Cat.

"I don't much care where," said Alice.

"Then it doesn't matter which way you go," said the Cat.

"So long as I get somewhere", Alice added as an explanation.

"Oh, you're sure to do that," said the Cat, "if you only walk long enough."

The instructor in question put up a slide. It was a mass of arrows all pointing in different directions.

His point was simple. To be successful, an organisation must create alignment and ensure that everybody is pulling in the same direction. It was such an obvious point that I wondered why on earth we were paying him to make it.

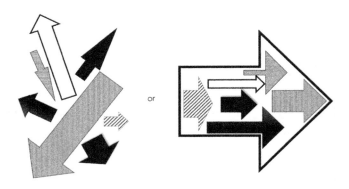

Figure 3: Coordinating Effort

Coordinating Effort

Thirty years on, I am a little wiser and more underwhelmed by the ways of the corporate world. Most organisations don't create alignment. They don't have a unifying purpose, or at least not one that anybody with imagination will get behind. Take Barnes & Noble, the US Book retailer, as an example. Their mission is *"To operate the best omni-channel specialty retail business in America, helping both our customers and booksellers reach their aspirations while being a credit to the communities we serve."*[15]

Like many organisations, their mission is all-encompassing, corporate and vague. It isn't particularly clear what they want to achieve, nor is it anything an employee will get excited about. Amazon's mission statement, by contrast, is more precise and compelling: *"We aim to be Earth's most customer-centric company."*[16]

If you want to become world-class, a crucial first step is to decide what you want to be world-class at. Hard on the heels of that decision comes a second question: "Is this something that will excite your employees?" It is difficult, if not impossible, to become world-class at something if nobody cares if you are successful. Some organisations are crystal clear about what they would like to achieve and have crafted simple, compelling statements that show exactly where they want to go.

The global FMCG conglomerate Unilever wants to *"Make Sustainable Life Commonplace."*[17] Lloyds Banking Group focuses on *"Helping Britain Prosper"*[18] and artfully pivoted to *"Helping Britain Recover"*[19] during the pandemic. Finally, the Dutch electronics group Philips aims to *"Improve people's health and well-being through meaningful innovation."*[20]

This may be rhetoric; it is one thing to say something and another to do it. But these organisations have a fighting chance of coordinating their employees' efforts.

There are plenty of other companies that are not nearly as focused. ExxonMobil Corporation is: *"… committed to being the world's premier petroleum and chemical manufacturing company. To that end, we must continuously achieve superior financial and operating results while adhering to high ethical standards."*[21]

Bluntly translated, that reads, "We want to be the best by making a lot of money and not doing anything immoral". How many of ExxonMobil's staff can remember, let alone get excited about, their mission?

Purposeful Organisations

When an organisation has a worthwhile purpose and follows through, the results can be staggering. Here are three organisations that have successfully aligned some (if not all) of their activity with a unifying goal.

Example 1: IKEA

When he died in 2018, Ingvar Kamprad was worth between $3 billion and $28 billion.* He was one of the 10 wealthiest men in the world.[22] Kamprad founded the company IKEA, which sells more

*The different valuations are a result of Kamprad's decision to put much of his fortune into trust to avoid tax though he still kept his billionaire status.

furniture than any other. It currently has 460 stores in 62 markets spread across every continent except Antarctica. Almost everyone in Europe setting up a home will visit one of IKEA's huge stores. Whilst there, they stock up on cheap, simple, stylish wardrobes, tables, crockery and lighting.

IKEA is so pervasive that it is claimed that one in 10 European babies is conceived in an IKEA bed, (though presumably not whilst it is still in the store).[23] Kamprad aimed to: *Offer a wide range of well-designed, functional home furnishing products at prices so low that as many people as possible will be able to afford them.*[24]

IKEA is the master of product design and supply. In the book *50 Things that Made the Modern Economy*, Tim Harford singles out IKEA for its "boringly effective systems".[25] The IKEA teams enhance their products continuously. They ensure they give customers exactly what they want without spending an unnecessary penny.

You may have drunk from a BANG mug at least once; IKEA has sold millions. The design path of the mug is buried somewhere deep in IKEA's headquarters in Älmhult, Sweden, but anecdotally it went a little like this:

First, the designers drew a simple, straightforward mug. IKEA's long-term supplier in Romania then produced them by the thousand. Next, they made the mug a little squatter and broader. Firing pottery takes a long time, and kilns are expensive equipment. The kiln is invariably the bottleneck of the production process. These changes meant more mugs would fit into each kiln. This increased throughput and reduced manufacturing costs. It also had the knock-on benefit of improving the number of mugs shipped on a pallet (up from 864 to 1,280), reducing distribution costs.[26]

Then the product team moved the handle up the side of the mug and added a flowerpot-style rim. The rim allowed customers to stack the mug far more effectively, saving cupboard space. It also saved distribution costs. Now the supplier could deliver 2,024 mugs on a single pallet.

Finally, they added a distinctive chip to every cup's bottom. The break in the rim acts as a drain when the mug is washed upside down in a dishwasher. It prevents pools of scummy water from accumulating. It also saves the cost of a sliver of clay on every mug. Since IKEA sold nearly 25 million BANG mugs every year, those slivers saved the company (and its customers) a mountain of clay.

Figure 4: BANG Mug

These incremental design changes reduced processing costs, material costs and shipping costs. They also gave their customers a mug they were happy with, judging by sales volumes. IKEA has since stopped making the BANG mug. Tastes move on, and they sell the FÄRGRIK mug instead. I imagine somebody in Sweden is busy wondering how many more they can squeeze onto a pallet.

Example 2: Whirlpool
When journalists discuss innovative businesses, they invariably start writing about technology. I've read plenty of articles where

the author gets frothy about their new phone and its fancy apps or the latest electric car. I have yet to hear anybody getting agitated about washing machines and microwave ovens. Domestic appliances or "white goods" do not set the imagination alight. In 1999 Whirlpool, one of the more prominent appliance manufacturers, confronted this reality.[27] They realised that customers saw their market as an undifferentiated "sea of white". A washing machine looks like a washing machine, no matter who made it.

In a rather unimaginative attempt to address the issue, Whirlpool's then-CEO David Whitwam decided the organisation needed to become the most innovative player in the market. To achieve that, the organisation needed *"Innovation from everyone, everywhere."*

Rather than spouting empty corporate talk, Whitwam appointed an Innovation Tzar and challenged her to make Whirlpool more innovative. Whilst everybody would like innovation, Whirlpool had the persistence to create it. Over the next 10 years, their Tzar developed and instigated a plethora of management initiatives to promote innovation:

- Innovation became a central topic in leadership development programmes.
- Every product development plan had to contain a "new to market innovation".
- A capital budget was set aside for innovation projects.
- Innovation boards allocated this capital and reviewed progress.
- Innovation was defined centrally (to prevent business units sucking up innovation capital).
- Employees were allowed to approach multiple innovation boards for investment.
- Six hundred innovation mentors were trained and appointed.

- Every employee went through innovation training.
- The senior management bonus was reconfigured to promote innovation.
- Quarterly business reviews had time specifically allocated to discuss innovation plans.
- An innovation portal was built that allowed employees access to innovation tools and data.
- Metrics were developed to measure innovation inputs, outputs and work in progress.

This host of initiatives didn't fall out of some master plan. They developed over time as the organisation hit obstacles and overcame problems. Whirlpool persisted with its approach for over a decade, constantly testing and learning what worked. The payback was striking. Innovation and new products became a substantial part of Whirlpool's revenues. In 2006, innovation accounted for roughly $1 billion of revenue. In 2007, this grew to $2.7 billion. By the following year, it was $4.0 billion.[28] The increasing revenue from innovation helped Whirlpool to maintain its top line. This was despite a major recession and a significant drop in the value of the housing market.

It is one thing for a competitor to reverse engineer a new washer or dryer. It is another thing for them to knock off a complex, interlinked management process and culture. The stream of new products was impressive, but the business capability that Whirlpool built was the real innovation.

Example 3: Nottinghamshire Libraries

A final example of a purposeful organisation is my local library. When my youngest daughter was five years old, she loved books and visiting the library. On one occasion, I took her to return her borrowed books, and the librarian told me that we were one short.

I asked my daughter where it was. "I left it on the train to Grannie's house", was her blunt response. I had visions of an overinflated fine and a black mark for disgraceful citizenship, so I asked the librarian how much I'd have to pay. She replied by asking my daughter's age. On discovering she was five, the librarian said, "Oh, there isn't a fine. If they are five or under, we don't impose one, and up to the age of 10, we only ask for half of the book's price."

It would have been effortless for the library to fleece me for the cost of some new stock, (this was an underfunded inner-city council outpost that needed all the money it could get), but they didn't. When I asked the librarian why not, she gave me a simple reason. The library service was clear about its purpose: *"To inspire the enjoyment of books and reading."*[29]

If an organisation aims to inspire the enjoyment of books and reading, an excellent place to start is letting children borrow books to read. The best way to convince parents to stop their children from borrowing books is to fine them whenever they lose one, as this is precisely what children do.

IKEA, Whirlpool and Nottinghamshire County Council's libraries are all clear about their purpose. But it isn't lip service; they back that up with projects, processes, policies, procedures, rules and regulations. They do what they say they are going to do. This all sounds obvious and trite, but having clarity of purpose and that purpose being meaningful and customer-focused is both nuanced and powerful.

A Little Bit of Theory

To understand why a clear purpose is essential to an organisation, we should discuss a little management theory (don't be alarmed – it won't take long). First, let's look at a branch of academia called systems thinking which explores how complex organisations, ecosystems, and economies behave.

"Systems thinking is a way of making sense of the world's complexity by looking at it in terms of wholes and relationships rather than splitting it into parts."[30]

The systems thinkers categorise systems (or, in this case, organisations) into three elements:

- **Components**: The team members and functions, the factories, warehouses, call centres and departments.
- **Interactions**: The information flows, rules, policies and procedures that hold the components together.
- **Purpose**: What the system is there to do.

Following that logic, there are three ways to change your organisation. You could change the components: open and close factories, or hire and fire people. The second option is to change the interactions between parts of your business: refine the way information flows, or change the rules. Finally, you could change its purpose: focus it on something different.

Managers invariably put their time and effort into changing components. They add new regional distribution centres, reorganise staff and find new suppliers to increase performance. Yet an improvement programme that only focuses on the individual parts of an organisation is doomed to failure. One of the gurus of systems thinking, Dr Russell L. Ackoff, explained why with one of his thought experiments.

The experiment suggests that you park every new car available on the market in an oversized garage. Next, find a team of the brightest automotive engineers and ask them to evaluate each vehicle to determine the best parts. They might say that the most robust transmission comes from a Range Rover, the most powerful engine can be found in a Lamborghini, the finest upholstery is in a Rolls Royce, and the safest impact systems are in a Volvo. Once they have determined the best parts, imagine using them all to create a "best-of-breed" automobile. Unfortunately, doing this won't build you a fantastic new car. You end up with a pile of parts that won't move anywhere. The reason is simple: the pieces don't fit.[31] *

Any systems integrator will tell you that if you buy a world-class customer management system or move to a new "class-leading" logistics supplier, 80% of the project effort is in integrating the new part into the business that you already have. Concentrating all your management effort on the individual components of your business won't take you very far.

The second level of the systems thinkers' model (interactions) is far more potent than the first (components). One of the most significant improvements I ever saw a business make was to initiate a robust "S&OP" process (sales and operations planning). It ensures that your business's supply and demand halves sit down once a month and talk to each other, doing wonders for customer service. Improving the data flows or interactions between a business's components, and allowing them to work better together is powerful stuff.

The final level of the systems thinker's model (purpose) is still more powerful. Managers rarely focus on their organisation's top-level objective. It sounds far too nebulous to be credible. Yet creating a unifying goal can have the most dramatic effect on how an organisation performs, as any sports fan can tell you.

In the world of competitive cricket, changing the game's purpose affected how it was played. There are two types of cricket

---

*Though he died in 2009, you can and should hear Dr Ackoff speak. Search online for "if Russ Ackoff had given a TED talk".

on television: test match cricket and twenty-20 cricket. The players (or components) and the rules (or interactions) are the same, but the aim of the game (or purpose) is different.

- In test match cricket, the batting side aims to score as many runs as possible with 11 batters.
- In twenty-20 cricket, the batting side aims to score as many runs as possible within 20 overs.

The players approach the game in very different ways, and that difference is palpable.[32]

"In Test cricket, players must be fit enough to spend many hours playing, and batsmen must be prepared to bat with patience for hours. Bowlers can attack more freely and have greater scope for setting fielders where they wish.

In twenty-20 cricket, bowlers must almost always bowl more defensively, as not conceding runs is more important than taking wickets. Batsmen can be more aggressive from the start, and boundaries are more frequent. Fielders are restricted where they may be placed on the field."

Changing the purpose of the game changes the way the game is played. Test cricket is a defensive game, and twenty-20 is an attacking game. The games are very different to watch. But the rules and players, interactions and components hardly change at all.

Like cricket, you can play with your business in different ways. You can run a company to look after its customers. Organisations that do that will find ways to charge customers less, invest in their assets and innovate. Alternatively, you can run a business to look after its profits. Organisations that do that will look for ways to charge their customers more, milk their assets and copy the competition. Both businesses will still have factories, call centres, accountants and marketing teams. Some interactions might change – the rules and the way information flows. But changing a business's purpose will change how it performs. Anybody who has worked for a company that has been milked will attest to that. Thinking of your organisation as a system helps explain why purpose is so powerful.

The Efficiency Paradox

The second bit of management theory suggests why not all purposes are equal. An externally focused business is far more likely to succeed than one that navel gazes and focuses on itself. Managers' obsession with optimising every part of their business, rather than worrying about either the interactions between departments or the external purpose they should be fulfilling, causes the "Efficiency Paradox":

Striving to make every part of the organisation as efficient as possible reduces the efficiency of the whole.

Nature abhors a vacuum, and the human psyche drives us to seek meaning and a sense of purpose. If people don't have a purpose or goal, they will create one. If you leave the different parts of a large organisation alone, you will soon discover that:

- Purchasing will *"Drive efficiency through the supply chain."*
- Operations will *"Strive to be the lowest cost provider."*
- Sales aim to *"Generate world-class revenues."*
- HR focus on *"Building human capital."*
- Finance will fall over themselves to *"Generate profitable growth."*

These goals are laudable and create vast numbers of initiatives. But as none of these aspirations defines where the business in totality wants to go, those schemes shoot off in different directions and at cross purposes. You'd imagine the net result would be zero, and the company goes nowhere, but it is worse than that. The outcome is negative as there is more time spent fighting over conflicting projects than improving the business. Each department is pulling in a different direction. Is it a surprise when the conversations between them become a little fractious? It is easy to see where the management trainer with the slide full of arrows got his inspiration.

In an article for the *Harvard Business Review*, Greg Satell highlights the Efficiency Paradox.[33] He demonstrates the effect with an example from General Stanley McChrystal's book, *Team of Teams*.[34] The general's soldiers were winning every battle against Al Qaeda in Iraq, yet he appeared to be losing the war. McChrystal realised that although his commandos and intelligence analysts were focused on performing their tasks to a world-class standard, they were so engrossed in their actions that they weren't looking at the entire organisation. He said that teams of commandos would carry out a raid and return with bags full of documents and computer hard drives. These would sit around because the analysts were too busy to look at them.

Likewise, an analyst would come up with tremendous insight, only to find that the teams on the ground had already headed off (at speed) in another direction. McChrystal increased the power and authority of his liaison officers and embedded specialists from one unit into another. Whilst this reduced the efficiency of the individual units, it made the whole organisation far more effective. Satell points out:

"If everyone is trained — and compensated — to focus on only their part of the task, the shared mission is lost. That's not a path to greater efficiency or profitability but oblivion."

An organisation should have a clear guiding purpose for everybody, not a host of splintered initiatives.

It's Not About You

Several high-profile organisations are exemplars of the power of purpose.

- Google aims to *"Organise the world's information and make it universally acceptable and useful."*[35]
- The Wikimedia Foundation wants to *"Empower and engage people around the world to collect and develop educational content under a free license or in the public domain, and to disseminate it effectively and globally."*[36]
- Netflix says it *"Want[s] to entertain the world. Whatever your taste, and no matter where you live."*[37]

These organisations have an external focus. They aim to do something for others. Consequently, they obsess about the service they deliver and the quality of their products. The alternative is to focus internally. Companies with an internal focus are preoccupied with stakeholder returns, profitability and efficiency.

Peter Drucker once wrote, "Efficiency is concerned with doing things right. Effectiveness is doing the right things."[38] Organisations exist to do something for someone, and they make money as a by-product of doing that something. Corporations with an external or customer focus worry about doing the right things for their customers; they focus on being effective. Organisations with an internal focus worry about doing things right; they focus on efficiency. Drucker played with this idea in several of his publications:

"Efficiency attempts to do things right; it deals with the ratio between input and output. Effectiveness is concerned with doing the right things; it deals with the quality rather than the quantity of results and output."

"Efficiency is not unimportant. A business can easily die of inefficiency. But no business can survive, let alone grow, because it is efficient."[39]

"There is surely nothing quite so useless as doing with great efficiency what should not be done at all."[40]

Many consultants have expanded on Drucker's thinking and developed the efficiency and effectiveness matrix to explain performance to their clients.

Figure 5: Efficiency and Effectiveness Matrix

Few companies fall neatly into one of the boxes, and most have moments of internal and external focus, so they stumble around the grid. However, it is easy to understand how an internally focused company can succumb to the Efficiency Paradox and fail. An internal focus will drive efficiencies but the company will loose sight of its raison d'être. Add to that the fact that every department strives to be the most efficient, and internal competition creeps in. Rival departments pushing their agendas will propel an organisation towards mediocrity, if not failure.

The Centre of Excellence

I once worked for an organisation that had an internal printing function, which amongst other roles looked after the company's photocopiers and printers. The area manager decided they would become a "Printing Centre of Excellence" with the lowest print costs possible. One of the ways he achieved this was to ban all colour photocopying (unless an executive had approved it).

The outcome was that managers were forced to make million-pound decisions whilst looking at complex PowerPoint slides and graphs where all the data was presented in mid-grey tones, and nobody could tell what they were looking at. It would be funny if it wasn't true.

Getting it Wrong

Whilst having a rallying cry or purpose statement is essential, it doesn't mean much if it is only words. The consultancy firm McKinsey & Company surveyed over 1,200 employees of US companies. The survey questioned both front-line staff and managers. The results showed that there was a massive gap between rhetoric and action.[41]

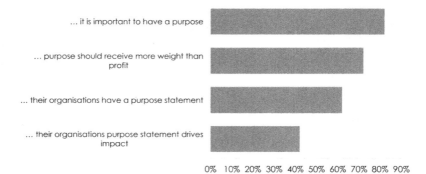

Figure 6: Purpose: Theory and Practice
(McKinsey and Co.)

Saying one thing and doing another is, at best, a waste of time and, at worst, hurts both staff and customers. Sears Roebuck and Co., the American retail chain, once proudly boasted, *"Satisfaction guaranteed or your money back."* But it was all talk. In 1992 the company was forced to refund $46.6 million to customers after the California Department of Consumer Affairs ran an 18-month undercover investigation.[42] The enquiry proved that Sears had systematically ripped off customers who used its car repair chain, billing for repairs that customers didn't need. On average, customers were overcharged by $223.

Imagine the impact of those conflicting words and behaviours on employees. It is unlikely that a mechanic working in one of those service centres would have been proud of his job. Nor would he have given the organisation every ounce of his discretional effort. Sears has since changed their slogan to *"Making Moments Matter"*. It is unclear how that has changed their actions.

The story of Sears Roebuck is a slam-dunk example of disingenuous management. The tale of Dean Foods Company (once the largest dairy producer in the US) is less clear cut. The stated aspiration of Dean Foods was a monument to internal focus.[43]

> *"The Company's primary objective is to maximize long-term stockholder value while adhering to the laws of the jurisdictions in which it operates and, at all times, observing the highest ethical standards."*

Dean Foods was another organisation that aimed to make as much money as possible without its directors being sent to jail.* In 2019, Dean Foods fell foul of changing consumer demands and filed for Chapter 11 bankruptcy protection. An analysis of how

---

* If not a carbon copy of Exxon Mobil's stated aims, there is an uncanny likeness. It is as if they were in the same business.

such a giant corporation failed highlighted several factors, including:

"... dropping fluid milk consumption, rising competition from private label and milk alternatives, and a complex company history with M&A gone wrong and financial missteps from which it never quite recovered."[44]

Opinions varied on the underlying cause. Kenneth Rosen, a partner at the law firm Lowenstein Sandler believed that the collapse was simply a reflection of a changing market.

"In the case of Dean Foods, you have a confluence of things that have sort of caused the tide to go out: less milk consumption, more vertical integration and a shift to private label. All of those things have caused a situation where, unless Dean Foods can become much more efficient, it can't compete. And that's what happened."

The Dean Foods CEO, Eric Beringause, voiced a very similar opinion blaming collapsing consumer demand.

"Despite our best efforts to make our business more agile and cost-efficient, we continue to be impacted by a challenging operating environment marked by continuing declines in consumer milk consumption."

But as analyst Bobby DeStefano pointed out, the market for plant-based dairy is growing and "People still need milk."

The retro-scope always provides perfect information, so I can easily speculate about a corporate collapse on the other side of the world. Yet it isn't hard to believe that Dean Foods fell into the Efficiency Paradox. The lack of an externally focused guiding purpose meant they became ineffective, missing out on what their customers wanted. It would be naive to claim that a strong customer focus would have saved the company, but it certainly would not have hurt.

Summary

Key Points

- Conflict and wasted effort will occur if an organisation hasn't got a single unifying purpose.
- Focused organisations can deliver outstanding results.
- Systems Thinking theory divides organisations into three parts: components, interactions and purpose.
- Most management efforts focus on improving components. Doing this alone doesn't work, as the components must interact.
- Changing the purpose of an organisation can have a significant effect.
- Internal functions will strive to drive independent departmental goals if left to their own devices.
- This results in conflicting agendas and the Efficiency Paradox, as optimising each part of a system destroys the effectiveness of the whole.
- Organisations with an external focus strive to do the right things; they try to be effective.
- Organisations with an internal focus strive to do things right; they try to be efficient.
- Effectiveness trumps efficiency. Only companies with a unifying customer-focused mission or purpose can hope to thrive.
- A purpose or mission statement is useless and demoralising if it is just words.

Actions

If you want your organisation to thrive, the parts should align on a clear customer focus.

- Write down and agree on the purpose of your team and organisation.
- It should be focused on delivering outside your team (not making your team more efficient).
- It should serve others.
- Your customers should care that you deliver it.
- It should be memorable, not management fluff.
- Your team should be inspired by it.
- If your organisation already has a clear purpose, yours should align with it.

An HR department might aim to deliver "the best support" to its internal customers in the wider business. This quickly begs the question of what the rest of the company believes is the best support. Southwest Airlines has a company promise to its employees:

> "Southwest will provide a stable work environment with equal opportunity for learning and personal growth. Employees will be provided the same concern, respect, and caring attitude within the organization that they are expected to share externally with every Southwest Customer."[45]

It is obvious what their HR department plan to do and why they believe it is important. Can you articulate your team's purpose with the same clarity? How do you know if they are achieving it if you can't?

You will get all you want in life if you help enough other people get what they want.

~ Zig Ziglar

Chapter 5:
Did You Hit Your Numbers?

Charles Goodhart and the Well-Established Tradition of Cheating

Once an organisation has decided upon its purpose, the next challenge is to create measures to see if it is achieving that aim. Organisations that don't measure performance can't see if they are getting better or worse. As they don't know how they are doing, they aren't able to manage. However, measures and performance are different. It is easy to believe that they go hand in glove, but that is far from the truth.

> *If you can't measure it, you can't manage it.*
>
> *~ Peter Drucker*

The Proxy for Performance

A ubiquitous management challenge is to ask, "Did you hit your numbers?" Anybody who runs an organisation knows they should hit their targets. It doesn't matter if it is a sales goal, a cost budget or a customer service statistic. If you've met your numbers, you've met your performance objectives.

To most managers, targets and performance are synonymous. Yet hitting a target is only a proxy for performance. If you type "proxy" into Google, it will give you this definition:

/'proksi/' noun

1. the authority to represent someone else, especially in voting.
   "Britons overseas may register to vote by **proxy**."

2. a figure that can be used to represent the value of something in a calculation. "the use of a US wealth measure as a **proxy** for the true worldwide measure."

Businesses often use the second definition. A proxy is a figure that represents the value of something. Economists might use unemployment rates as a proxy for the strength of the job market, or public health officials might use infant mortality as a proxy for the quality of healthcare.

Proxies are helpful because they indicate what is happening in a complex system without looking at every aspect. It is tough to measure absolute performance. If your New Year's resolution is to get fit, plenty of measures will show if you are hitting the goal. You could measure strength, endurance, weight, blood pressure, body fat and flexibility. That is before you start to count the number of cigarettes you smoke and the units of alcohol you consume. To make things easier, we use proxy measures. Instead of worrying about our BMI (body mass index) and taking blood sugar and cholesterol tests, we aim to "lose a bit of weight". These measures help guide us and are easy to get, but they are not the same as performance as they only measure a single dimension.

Business performance is every bit as multifaceted as our health. We must please customers, stakeholders, regulators and employees. We strive to reduce costs and time to serve, whilst increasing revenues and customer retention. Instead of trying to measure all those things, managers choose something simple to measure linked to what they wish to achieve and then hand it to their subordinates as a performance target. But these objectives and targets are not performance. They are only proxies for it.

> *The map is not the territory.*
>
> *~ Alfred Korzybski*

Measures and Targets

The fact that we struggle to measure every aspect of performance wouldn't be an issue if it weren't for the fact that we use measures and targets interchangeably. It is deeply ingrained into our collective management psyche that you should never present a measure without an accompanying target. However, adding a target is the management equivalent of opening Pandora's box.

In 1975 the British economist Charles Goodhart criticised the monetary policy of Margaret Thatcher's government.[46] In his paper, Goodhart wrote:

"Any observed statistical regularity will tend to collapse once pressure is placed upon it for control purposes."

This point has since been simplified to what has become known as Goodhart's Law:

"When a measure becomes a target, it ceases to be a good measure."

Or, to put it more prosaically, **when a measure becomes a target, people will cheat** to hit it. If you only take one point away from this book, that is the most critical.

The management ethos in most organisations revolves around "Management by Objectives". People at all levels in the organisation are given targets to hit. The CEO must meet a profit number, and the lowliest call centre agent is presented with a call-handle-time target. The prevailing wisdom is to link these targets to rewards and penalties; a nice fat bonus for those who do well or the threat of job loss for those who don't. The "if, then" approach is relied upon to motivate staff to hit their objectives. This dynamic is invariably combined with an artfully constructed cascade of targets that roll from the top of the organisation to the bottom in the belief that doing so will make the business excel.

This mechanism fails as there are many ways an individual or an organisation can hit their target. Most have lots to do with perception but vanishingly little to do with performance.

Option 1: Argue About the Data

In the movie *East is East*, there is a great line. Crude but great…

> "And what d'you think I do in there morning till night? Counting mushy fuckin' peas?"*

Andrew Dilnot and Michael Blastland picked up on the idea in their book, *The Tiger That Isn't*.[47] The problem with counting mushy peas is that it is hard to determine what a mushy pea is. How do you define one?

- Is it a specific size?
- Does it have to be a particular shade of green?
- What proportion of a whole pea should it be?
- What about the shape?
- Or sloppiness?
- Or texture?

It is tough to say when a mushy pea is a mushy pea. Yet peas are only the start of the measurement problem. Other things are far more critical, such as Covid-19 death rates.

In 2020, the BBC News ran an article discussing how different countries were measuring and reporting the spread of Covid-19 during the height of the pandemic.[48] Countries tried different policies and processes to fight the virus. Understanding how effective the other countries' strategies were at combatting the

---

*If you aren't from the UK and don't know what a mushy pea is, then you are gastronomically bereft and should try them if you visit us. Be warned – they are so good that we have none left to export.

disease was essential. The knowledge was a matter of life and death. But like mushy peas, there wasn't a standardised way of counting Covid-19 deaths. Professor Sir David Spiegelhalter (a statistician from Cambridge University) said that trying to rank different countries to decide which was performing better or worse was "a completely fatuous exercise".

The first problem was agreeing when Covid-19 was the cause of death. Each country produced daily headline metrics, but they counted deaths differently. Whilst there was no disputing that somebody was dead, the first question was, where did they die? England only counted Covid-19 deaths in hospitals (until Thursday, the 29th of April 2021, when they changed their mind and started to include those in care homes as well). In contrast, France and Germany had always included care homes in their numbers.

Similarly, the next question was whether somebody died from Covid-19. Was it necessary for the deceased to have tested positive for the virus? The Germans thought it was, yet the Belgians were more relaxed and said that a doctor's suspicions were enough. To further confuse matters, the UK's daily figures only included the deaths of those who had tested positive, yet the weekly totals included suspected cases.

Another question was whether the virus was the leading cause of death or whether there was another issue. Both my mother-in-law and godmother died of Covid-19, but they were both in their eighties with other health problems. Was Covid-19 the cause of their death, or did it ease them on their way?

The counting and comparison problems became more pronounced as the authorities included additional levels of statistical sophistication. Take the question of the death rate per head of the population. How do you compare an African country with a young population with a western country with an ageing one? If a country had a heavy testing regime and more confirmed cases, does that mean it had more deaths from the disease, or was it better at spotting those who had it? Even relatively simple comparisons, such as the UK versus the Republic of Ireland, were fraught. Ireland has a rural population, whereas the UK is far more urban, and the virus spread rapidly when there was close contact. Was comparing County Donegal with County Durham fair (or helpful)?

Just because somebody states a number doesn't mean you can believe what they say. Was the number of deaths reported by the Chinese authorities an accurate number? China, the source of the virus, had meagre numbers, even after they revised their death toll up by 50% in Wuhan, the suspected source of the virus. Political factors came into play. According to the North Korean authorities, the country was the safest place in the world, as they only had one confirmed case. But as they also recorded six deaths, the death rate was 600%. Read into that what you will.[49]

Measuring things is difficult. Any manager who wishes to avoid an awkward conversation about a performance target can easily argue about the data. A poor performance plus disputed data can quickly become a good performance.

Option 2: Change the Measure

My daughter went to university in 2021 to study maths and computer science. She is a bright girl. However, her "brightness" level has become a sore topic at home. When I got my A-Level results in 1986, I received an A grade, a D and an E. My daughter, however, got two A grades and a third A*. This result, by her reckoning, makes her super clever and more to the point (and her amusement), it makes me an intellectual pygmy.

An academic paper came to my rescue.[50] 2021 was the year that the UK Government gave way to public opinion over the exam marking system. Students hadn't been able to attend school during the pandemic, and there was intense political pressure to include teachers' assessments of their pupils' performance in exam scores to ensure grades were fair. The summary of the report says:

> "[This was] a recipe for inflation. The grade received was to be the highest of the teacher's predicted grade; the Ofqual calculated grade or, in the case of Wales, the AS grade achieved in 2019. This led to:
> - The first ever 100% pass rate.
> - The highest ever percentage of A*/A grades.
> - A bonanza for subjective subjects.
> - The biggest ever gap in favour of girls at A*/A."

My daughter read the report and claimed it was a lot of excitement about nothing. The data, however, shows another picture. Until 1987, the A-level pass rate was stable as it was set at predetermined proportions, with the top 10% receiving A-grade passes. However, since then, the system for awarding grades has changed four times.

- From 1987 onwards, the quotas were replaced by a standards-based system. Anybody who met a predetermined level would receive an A grade regardless of how many there were.
- In 2010, Ofqual was established to regulate the qualifications. They devised a statistical method to keep the grades comparable between 2011 and 2019.
- In 2020 the pandemic hit, and the government used an algorithm to calculate grades.
- The algorithm was so politically unpopular that in 2021 the government bowed to public pressure and allowed teachers' predicted grades into the mix.

These changes had a dramatic effect on results. I have (for my daughter's benefit) highlighted the years I did my A-Levels, and she did hers.

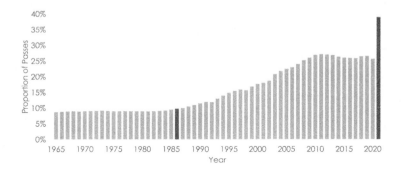

Figure 7: UK A-Level Pass Rates at A and A*

The purpose of this little lesson is not to point out to my daughter that she had it easy (OK, yes, I did say that), but to show that if you keep changing how you measure something, it is challenging to see what (if anything) has got better. There is endless heat and light generated in the UK educational system by the annual exam results, but what is the point of the exams? Is it to show that education is improving? Is it there to identify the best students? Is it to measure the performance of schools? Or perhaps it is to identify poor teachers? The only real lesson I can take is that it is unwise to let politicians (or managers) dabble with performance measures, especially if they have their reputations at risk.

Option 3: Distort the Data

As a small boy, the most exciting thing in the world was a day trip to London with my father. I was brought up in a field in deepest, darkest North Yorkshire. The big smoke was terrific as it had museums, skyscrapers, underground trains, toy shops, galleries and ice cream. Where I came from, all there was to look at was sheep. Before we got off the train at Kings Cross, my father always gave me the same advice:

"If you get lost, find a police officer, and ask him for help. You can always trust a police officer."

It transpires that my father was wrong. In September 1996, Detective Superintendent Peter Coles resigned from Nottinghamshire Constabulary. He had blown the whistle on the force's crime recording practices, and his position had become untenable.[51] In a report to his senior commanders, Coles warned:[52]

"A culture of good results is burgeoning, paying scant regard to the methods employed by junior officers to serve the ambition of their seniors ... The greatest danger is that we appear to believe in our own publicity and accept the hypocrisy as the truth."

The cause of his angst was a pair of targets the UK Government had introduced to increase police effectiveness. One was to reduce crime levels, and the other was to increase detection rates. Superintendent Coles accused his superiors of cheating to hit them both. The subsequent enquiry found that:

"The true picture of recorded and detected crime was being suppressed and distorted."

Nottinghamshire Constabulary was found guilty of "cuffing" and "nodding".[53]

Cuffing is the art of making a crime disappear up the cuff of a policeman's sleeve. The police achieved this by splitting major crimes into minor ones. A burglary would become a combination

of theft and assault (which the statistics rated less severely).
Likewise, thefts of handbags became cases of lost property. By
cuffing these and other crimes this way, they fell outside the
defined measures that the force had to report to the Home Office.
The month before Detective Superintendent Coles' resignation,
Nottinghamshire Chief Constable Peter Green claimed:[54]

> "In the past 12 months, burglary has fallen by 24 per cent,
> robbery by 25 per cent and car crime by 18 per cent."

The enquiry ultimately discovered that serious crime in the
county had actually increased by 1,387 cases. This finding was at
stark odds with the numbers that the police force had reported to
central government. They claimed that serious crime had fallen by
7,788 incidents.

As well as reducing the number of recorded crimes,
Nottinghamshire Constabulary used a similar method, nodding, to
improve its detection rates. They did this by persuading criminals
to nod to other offences that should be taken into consideration,
guaranteeing offenders that their admissions would not incur any
extra penalty, plus the promise of a positive word in court when
the time came. On one occasion, the police persuaded an 11-year-
old girl they had caught shoplifting to admit to another 80
offences, even though there wasn't any evidence to support this
claim. Another criminal confessed to five burglaries, which he
couldn't have done as he was in prison at the time. The enquiry
also found "detected crimes" that weren't even "recorded crimes".
[55]

Nottingham isn't a bad town. I have lived in the city for 25
years. Contrary to what you might read in the papers, it isn't
"Shottingham", the gun crime capital of the UK. I prefer to believe
it is the "Queen of the Midlands". In my hometown's defence, it is

worth recounting the tale of the Kent Police. Ten years before the Nottingham debacle, Constable Ron Walker went to Scotland Yard with allegations of corruption within Kent Constabulary. He accused 60 of his colleagues of fabricating crime figures. The Metropolitan Police's Serious Crime Squad raided 13 Kent police stations. When they arrived at Kent Constabulary's headquarters in Gravesend (some 30 miles from Scotland Yard), they found that all but one of the documents they were looking for had been shredded. Was this a case of a management coverup, or simply that the Serious Crime Squad got lost on their way out of London?

If you google "police manipulate crime figures", the target-focused British Constabulary make a good showing, but they are not alone. There are hits for New York and Buckeye, Arizona. You will also find stories from as far afield as Australia and South Africa. Sadly, you can't trust the police to tell the truth anywhere.

As all managers know, creative accounting works wonders if you have a difficult target to hit.

Option 4: Distort the System

In December 2017, Oliver Schmidt, a general manager for Volkswagen (VW), was sentenced to seven years in prison and fined $400,000.[56] He had been on holiday and was flying back to his home in Germany when federal agents arrested him in the men's room at an airport in Florida. Schmidt had been the senior executive in Volkswagen's engineering and environmental office in Michigan, where he was responsible for VW's emissions programme. He was found guilty of concealing deceptive software in nearly 60,000 diesel vehicles sold in the United States. Sean Cox, the Detroit judge who sentenced Schmidt, said:

> "It is my opinion that you are a key conspirator in this scheme to defraud the United States ... You saw this as

your opportunity to shine ... and climb the corporate
ladder at VW."

Schmidt was the most senior Volkswagen executive
prosecuted for their role in the "diesel dupe" affair. His bosses
weren't prepared to travel to the US and face the music. However,
they didn't get an easy ride in Germany. The scandal wreaked
havoc in Volkswagen Audi's corporate headquarters. Martin
Winterkorn, the group's chief executive, resigned after admitting
that Volkswagen had "broken the trust of our customers and the
public."[57]

The source of the drama was a decision by Volkswagen to
develop a software solution that helped them meet stringent
nitrous oxide (or NOx) emission targets that the US Environmental
Protection Agency (EPA) had placed upon diesel cars.

The proven way to hit these tight emission standards was to
utilise a system that Mercedes-Benz had developed called
"BlueTEC". This technology added a urea compound into the
exhaust system to reduce harmful gases. Engineers at VW thought
the technology was bulky, expensive and high maintenance, so
they developed the "lean NOx trap" instead. Unfortunately, the
system didn't work well enough, so VW technologists applied a
software "solution" to the engine management system.

The NOx test in the US was stringent but not sophisticated.
Officials measured emissions by putting cars onto rollers in test
centres and leaving them to run at a defined speed for a specific
time. Volkswagen programmed its cars to recognise these
conditions. When they did, the engine management system would
change the fuelling regime to minimise emissions. Under normal
road conditions, these settings would have compromised the car's
drivability, but as no one was driving, no one noticed.

The wheel fell off (excuse the pun) when a group of scientists decided to perform independent on-road tests. They tried three cars: a BMW X5, a VW Passat and a VW Jetta. The BMW passed the test with flying colours, yet the two Volkswagens emitted up to 40 times more NOx than permitted.

The authorities started a full investigation. When the EPA finally located the code "managing" the engine, they discovered that the software engineers had disingenuously labelled it "acoustic condition". VW installed the software between 2009 and 2015. Over this period, Volkswagen sold 8.5 million cars in Europe and half a million in the US.[58] Ultimately, the issue became a legislative bloodbath. The total cost of the affair will never be known. I suspect even German accountants, with their undoubted precision, have given up trying to count it all. However, it has been estimated that the emissions scandal cost Volkswagen €31.3 billion in fines, settlements and legal costs.[59]

This tale of corporate corruption and greed shows that even commercial giants aren't above distorting the system instead of improving it when there is a target with a significant financial reward.

Option 5: Improve Performance

Improving performance is the hardest of the five ways to hit a business target. To do it, managers must develop a sound understanding of the system they are working with and then go through all the pain of learning, building capability and removing waste. It also means they must collaborate with their colleagues and suppliers, open themselves up to failure and be brutally honest with their bosses.

Improving performance is tricky. The easiest way to get on in a large organisation is to use one of the other methods. This statement may sound cynical, but history repeatedly shows that if managers challenge their employees with a target and reinforce it with a large incentive, the employees will cheat to hit the target. The phenomenon is so widespread that it has a name, a "Perverse Incentive", and its own Wikipedia entry.

Perverse Incentives

The UK's National Health Service (NHS) has a slang term for some of the proxy targets it has received from the UK Government; they are known as "P45 targets".[60] It implies that a target is so politically important that you will lose your job if you fail to hit it. (In the UK, a P45 is a document you receive from your employer if you are made redundant).

Christopher Hood, a professor at Oxford University, investigated the effectiveness of the government's approach to managing the NHS and concluded that the medical profession is very adept at meeting P45 targets.[61]

One target specified that patients shouldn't wait more than 48 hours to see a general practitioner. In response, the doctors stopped taking appointments to see anybody more than two days in advance. Goodbye, waiting list.

Another target challenged hospital managers to ensure all emergency admissions were given a bed within 12 hours. The managers responded by taking the wheels off the rolling stretchers (gurneys) the patients were lying on, instantly converting them into "beds".

There is nothing new in any of this. Combining a measure with a target and an incentive invariably creates perverse outcomes. At the height of the British Empire, the governors of Colonial India were very worried about the number of cobras in Delhi. (No self-respecting bureaucrat likes venomous snakes). The governors came up with a plan. They offered a reward for every snake that the public killed. The incentive was a massive success. Dead snakes arrived by the basketful at government buildings.

As the governors hoped, the number of snakes in the city dwindled, and so did the number of dead cobras being handed over. Some bounty hunters, however, were better than others at catching snakes. They kept on trapping them, killing them and claiming their bounty. Eventually, the British cottoned onto the fact that the snake catchers weren't finding the snakes; they were breeding them. Once the British Government got wise to this, they stopped the programme. The snake breeders let their snakes go free, and the population of wild cobras in the city increased.[62]

A very similar thing happened elsewhere in Asia. In 1902, under French Colonial rule in Vietnam, a comparable programme was instigated to reduce the population of rats. The Vietnamese bounty hunter had to present the rat's tail to receive payment. It was a clear target and incentive. Eventually, the French noticed that there were lots of rats roaming the city without tails. The bounty hunters had caught the rats, lopped off their tails and then let them go again. A rat without a tail can still breed; it would have been foolish of the rat catchers to kill off such a lucrative revenue stream.[63]

Management Complicity

Detective Superintendent Peter Coles resigned from Nottinghamshire Constabulary. He had 35 years of service, held a Queen's Police Medal and was the most senior operational detective in the county. When he left, the Nottinghamshire police force privately suggested that his reason for resigning was that Coles was a frustrated man who had become embittered by his lack of progress. They claimed that he had quit of his own free will and not in protest. Yet the Bedfordshire investigators saw it differently. Their view was that:

"If Mr Coles had not made his complaint, judging by the force's apathy and inaction that followed it, it is doubtful whether any action would ever have been taken."

It takes a strong man to stand up to that level of organisational pressure. Anybody who has worked in a large corporation can recount examples of employees being given a simple numerical target with a big incentive (a carrot or a stick) and the staff member cheating to hit that target. The more unachievable and arbitrary the target, or the more substantial the incentive, the more deception will occur. Loaded targets always result in cheating, and cheating always drives ineffectiveness. Yet even though we all know it happens, managers continue to use target setting to "drive performance". There are only two ways to explain why:

- Managers are stupid.
- Managers know what goes on but turn a blind eye to it. They are too busy basking in the glory of smashed targets.

> *What is common sense isn't common practice.*
>
> *~ Stephen Covey*

Your organisation may use all the tools and techniques invented in the improvement armoury. Yet, if it insists on setting individual targets with incentives, it will never be better than average. And it will only be average because most other organisations are similarly deluded. On a positive note, if you change your approach, you will quickly stand head and shoulders above your competition.

Fear invites wrong figures. Bearers of bad news fare badly. To keep his job, anyone may present to his boss only good news.

~ W. Edwards Deming

The Right Way to Use a Measure

Returning to Peter Drucker's statement, "If you can't measure it, you can't manage it", there are two ways to interpret how Drucker thought we should manage with measures.

The first is to use the measure to command-and-control behaviour with targets and incentives. I hope I have explained the folly of that approach.

The alternative is to use the measure to learn. When used well, measures can provoke questions and demonstrate the effect of changes to processes and systems.

One man who understood how potent measures can be to help develop understanding and rectify a dismal situation was the physician Dr John Snow.[64] During the 19th century, cholera was one of the deadliest diseases to affect Britain. This was before the development of germ theory. Doctors and public health officials believed that a "miasma" carried by the bad smells produced by rotting organic matter caused the spread of the disease.

In August 1854, there was a devastating outbreak in Soho in central London. Within three days, 127 people died.[65] Snow described the episode as "the most terrible outbreak of cholera which ever occurred in this kingdom." It was the third wave of the disease to plague the city in just over 20 years. Soho was particularly badly hit as it had a nasty problem with filth. There had been a large influx of people, and the area's sewage system amounted to little more than a collection of cesspits under individual houses.

With the help of a local clergyman, Reverend Henry Whitehead, Snow spent time with residents, measuring the extent of the outbreak. He discovered that the disease wasn't spreading through the city uniformly, but that there was variation in death rates, with some areas being struck severely whilst others escaped unscathed.

After plotting the deaths onto a street map, Snow noticed that the disease attacked houses that took their drinking water from a pump on Broad Street (now known as Broadwick Street). He concluded that contaminated water from the local well transmitted the disease.[66] Snow's data convinced the Saint James parish authorities to disable the pump by removing its handle and stopping inhabitants from taking water from it. This intervention, in turn, curtailed the outbreak. Officials later discovered that the sewage from a nearby cesspit had polluted the water. Snow's use of measures and investigation into variable death rates was an archetypal test-and-learn cycle.

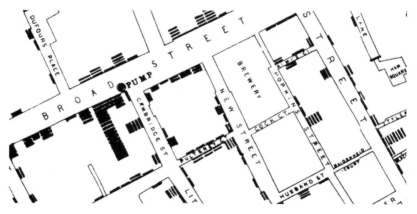

Figure 8: Dr John Snow's Cholera Map

As with all breakthroughs, the bureaucracy didn't universally accept Snow's findings. After the epidemic had subsided, officials replaced the Broad Street pump handle. Leaving it off would have meant they agreed with Snow's theory and indirectly also accepted the oral-faecal disease transmission method, which was too unpleasant for most people to entertain. However, ultimately Snow's discovery profoundly impacted the development of sewage systems and public health in London and, arguably, worldwide. Using a measure to control people will get you one set of outcomes. Using it to improve will get you another.

> *If you can't measure it, you can't improve it.*
>
> *~ Lord Kelvin*

Summary
Key Points
- You can't improve performance if you don't know how you are doing. Performance improvement and measurement go hand in hand.
- Measures are only a proxy. It is easy to beat a measure and much more complicated to improve performance.
- You should use measures for learning and not to control people.
- Understanding the causes of variation generates learning and improvement.

To reinforce an earlier point, if you only take one thing away from this book, please let it be this. **If you use measures as targets to control individuals and add a big incentive, they will cheat.** They always have, and they always will. The bigger the carrot or stick, the more dysfunctional your organisation will become.

Actions
- If you use measures and targets to control employees' performance and productivity, critically evaluate their effect.

- If the targets you set result in dysfunctional behaviour, stop using them. You are better off without them.

Part 3.

Promoting Learning

Chapter 6:
How We Learn

As Easy as Falling Off a Bicycle

When my daughter turned five, I bought her a bicycle. We took her for her first-ever bicycle ride that weekend, and my wife and I went to war.

- **Mummy logic**: The little darling needs stabilisers so she doesn't fall off and hurt herself.
- **Daddy logic**: Take the little brat to the top of a hill and give her a shove. It never hurt me.

Views became entrenched, battle lines were drawn, tempers flared… Of course, Mummy was wrong, but Daddy wasn't entirely right either. The only way to learn how to ride a bike is to fall off it and get back on again. By understanding what doesn't work, children eventually find out what does. If a child has stabilisers, they will never fall off and learn. Sooner or later, they must remove the stabilisers so they might as well get on with it. Nobody ever learnt to ride a bicycle without repeatedly falling off (or failing).

The contentious point in this argument is that you can't learn anything new unless you fail.* If you try something that works, all you have done is confirmed what you already thought to be true. The experience didn't teach you anything new.

---

*It is possible to learn from success, but only if that success is unexpected and challenges previously held beliefs. Unfortunately, in my personal experience, unexpected failure has occurred far more often than unexpected success.

My wife pointed out that my precise, logical argument had a minor flaw. My daughter was unlikely to get back on her bicycle if I had just launched her from the top of Scafell Pike and she had broken her neck. It is sensible to limit the downside of failure. Falling off a bicycle is a good thing. Just avoid doing it at speed.

The Learning Cycle

There is a formal mechanism for learning from your mistakes. It is called the "Scientific Method", "Learning Cycle" or "Plan, Do, Check Act" (PDCA), which is how scientists run experiments to increase knowledge. There are four stages to the PDCA process:

The first stage is to plan. Something will happen that sparks an idea, or an event makes you take note. Let's take, as an example, a car that won't start. This will lead to countless theories (or hypotheses) about what is wrong with it. Perhaps it has run out of petrol, or the battery is flat. Maybe it has had an oil leak and the engine has seized. Take your favourite idea and plan an experiment to test it. If the hypothesis is that the battery is flat, the planned experiment is to jump-start the car with the neighbour's van. If the theory is correct, the vehicle should start.

The second stage is to do the experiment or run the test. Invite your neighbour over and hand him the jump leads.

Stage three is to check or evaluate what happened and see if your hypothesis was correct. Did the car start? Once you know how the experiment went, you have either learnt something or reinforced what you already knew.

Finally, act or iterate on the knowledge. That action might be to:

- Stop the cycle and move on to the next problem – the test resolved the issue and the car started.
- Move on what you have learnt – check to see if you need a new battery or buy a home charger.

- Revise your thinking and move on to a new plan – maybe the car has run out of fuel.

This approach is common sense, but many organisations are poor at learning. Instead of PDCA they fall back on "Do, Do, Do, Do".

- **Do**: Make an improvement.
- **Do**: Change a process.
- **Do**: Implement some training.
- **Do**: Install a system.

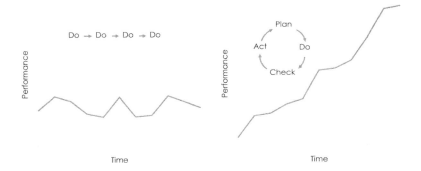

Figure 9: Do, Do, Do, Do or PDCA

When they have been through the four Dos, they keep right on doing. The method has the advantage that managers feel they are making progress, and it is clear that they are doing something. Bosses love to see progress. But because there isn't any measurement or reflection, there is very little learning, and no increase in performance or productivity.

I Feel the Need, the Need for Speed

Learning cycles aren't limited to science; they also have a place in warfare. Military history shows there were two ways to win a battle. Either recruit a bigger army or build more powerful weapons.

There were only two variables that mattered – size and power. The number of soldiers and the calibre of their guns were good indicators of who would win. Conflicts were wars of attrition, and military might was everything. The First World War trenches that run through northern France and Belgium demonstrate the point admirably.

The military strategist, Colonel John Boyd, was a fighter pilot in the Korean war. He realised that there was a missing factor in the equation – speed. If numbers were equal, it wasn't the biggest, most powerful fighter planes that won dogfights but the smaller, more agile ones. Boyd developed the "OODA loop" to help train US fighter pilots.[67] OODA stands for:

- **Observe**: Gather data, and see what your opponent is doing.
- **Orientate**: Process that data to get meaning from it.
- **Decide**: Work out what the best course of action is.
- **Act**: Play out your decision.

The OODA loop is, in many ways, like the scientific method (Plan, Do, Check and Act) in that both cycles rely on feedback. In a dogfight, the ability to run through the cycle quickly and repeatedly determines success. A pilot who can act faster than his opponent or "get inside his loop" puts the opponent on the back foot, constantly reacting to what happened, or better still, to a situation that no longer exists.

> *He who can handle the quickest rate of change survives.*
>
> *~ Colonel John Boyd*

The rate at which a pilot can make decisions and learn from them is critical in air (and military) supremacy. Learning loops work for the military and also in business.

Sex and Soap Powder

There is a soap powder factory near Liverpool. Unilever owns it and they make brands like Persil and Surf. In that factory, the workers mix a bunch of ingredients: water softeners, enzymes, bleach, detergent and water. Then they pump the resulting slurry through a spray nozzle at high pressure and temperature. As the slurry passes through the outlet, the water evaporates and leaves behind a powder that looks like snow. Finally, operators in the factory take that powder, put it in a box and sell it.

The people who do this for a living had a problem – the nozzle kept blocking. Their soap powder was too big, small, dry or wet. If you make soap powder, the last thing you need is a nozzle clogged with sludge. It gets costly very quickly. Making soap powder is a lucrative business, and Unilever is a wealthy company, so they decided to put together two teams of experts to fix the problem.

The first set of experts were chemical engineers. They had qualifications in heat exchange mechanisms and applied mathematics. If fluid dynamics was top of your list, these were the people to have in the room. The second set of experts were evolutionary biologists. For my sins, I was once an evolutionary biologist. People like me know about sex (only the theory, not the practice) and nothing about making soap powder. Unilever was interested in two things: they wanted to fix the problem, but they were also very interested in understanding which of the two teams had the best approach to solving it.

The engineers investigated the problem, wrote equations and held meetings. Then they designed and built a solution, and implemented it. It was a better nozzle, but the problems prevailed.

The biologists took a different tack. They weren't experts in production engineering. All they knew about was evolution. They took the nozzle and made 10 copies, but they weren't identical. Some were fatter, and some were thinner. Some were taller, and some were shorter. Some had notches in them, whilst others had grooves. They were all slightly different. The biologists then pumped soap slurry through the different nozzles until they blocked, then looked at the results. They measured the quality and output, and determined which one of the 10 nozzles was the best. The scientists threw away nine failures, took the best nozzle and made 10 copies of that one. Again, each had minor differences. They repeated the trial-and-error process for 45 generations. After they had failed 449 times, the biologists stopped. They had developed a nozzle that was substantially better.[68]

The exercise is a case study in organisational learning. The biologists ran through the test-and-learn cycle, and, in line with Colonel Boyd's thinking, they did it quickly. We live in a complex world. We can't hope to understand everything. Success comes from trying, not debating.

An organisation that wants to get better should run (small) experiments and accept that they are going to have failures. It should then lock in the knowledge from each failure and repeat.

An Intellectual Hop and a Cultural Leap

It doesn't take a genius to see how the OODA loop or the scientific method applies to other activities. If an organisation can improve faster than its opponents in sports, litigation, politics or business, it will leave its competitors reeling. Learning and adapting quickly is a competitive advantage, yet many of our organisations are far from agile. Meetings often fail to conclude, and issues are "kicked upstairs" so somebody on a higher pay grade can pass judgement. Endless committees do nothing for an organisation's ability to whirl through the learning loop faster than its competition.

If an organisation wants to learn quickly, it must be prepared to force decisions down through the ranks so more people can make them. Fast devolved decision-making requires a clear purpose, a cooperative working environment, flat structures, aligned objectives and trust. Only some organisations (or their managers) are prepared to do that. The rest prefer to have risk and control frameworks, quorate committees and senior management reviews. The command-and-control mechanisms employed by large organisations stifle learning. It is far better to make the wrong decision, learn from it and move on than not make a decision. After all, if you get it wrong, you can always back it out.

Summary
Key Points
- Productivity only rises if an organisation learns something new and applies it.
- Learning comes when things don't happen as we expect. This is invariably from failure (unexpected success is lovely but rare).
- Lots of small failures are much better than one large one.
- The scientific method (PDCA) formalises the learning process.
- The faster you fail, the quicker you improve.

Actions
- Pick an issue and run through the learning cycle with it.
- Plan an experiment.
- Do a trial.
- Check to see what happened. Did things work out as you expected?

- Act on the knowledge, lock in the improvement or plan another trial.
- Repeat.

Chapter 7:
Barriers to Learning

The Self-Defeating Management Ego

Whilst organisational learning is something every manager will pay lip service to, many cultural and attitudinal barriers prevent it. These obstacles stem from some deeply held management beliefs.

- Belief 1: Information is power.
- Belief 2: Managers know best.
- Belief 3: You should reward success and punish failure.
- Belief 4: Big and strategic beats small and tactical.
- Belief 5: You must be at the cutting edge.
- Belief 6: The action is at head office.
- Belief 7: Problems are a sign of weakness.

These beliefs, at the core of many a manager's ego and self-image, devastate an organisation's ability to learn.

> *It is what we know already that often prevents us from learning.*
>
> *~ Claude Bernard*

Information is Power

Managers and politicians alike are keen to protect their positions and promote themselves. One of the ways a manager can do this is by restricting the flow of information, being very careful how they "manage the message", and only sharing information on a need-to-know basis. Whilst this may be good for the manager, it isn't good for the organisation.

In her book, *Thinking in Systems*, Donella H. Meadows recounts an intriguing story.[69]

Electric Meters in Dutch Houses

"Near Amsterdam, there is a suburb of single-family houses all built at the same time, all alike. Well, nearly alike. For unknown reasons it happened that some of the houses were built with the electric meter down in the basement. In other houses, the electric meter was installed in the front hall.

These were the sort of electric meters that have a glass bubble with a small horizontal metal wheel inside. As the household uses more electricity, the wheel turns faster and a dial adds up the accumulated kilowatt-hours.

During the oil embargo and energy crisis of the early 1970s, the Dutch began to pay close attention to their energy use. It was discovered that some of the houses in this subdivision used one-third less electricity than the other houses. No one could explain this. All houses were charged the same price for electricity; all contained similar families.

The difference, it turned out, was in the position of the electric meter. The families with high electricity use were the ones with the meter in the basement, where people rarely saw it. The ones with low use had the meter in the front hall where people passed, the little wheel turning around, adding up the monthly electricity bill many times a day."

The story makes a neat point. A simple way to enhance performance is to let people have the information they need in a straightforward, easy-to-read, readily visible format. Then let them do the rest. If your staff don't have the data that tells them how they are doing, they can't act on it.

In his book *Outliers*, Malcolm Gladwell claimed you need 10,000 hours of practice to master something.[70] Critics of his 10,000-hour rule will tell you that whilst practice is essential, it isn't the only factor. One critical issue is feedback. A triage nurse on a casualty ward who has worked for 10,000 hours will have perfected her judgement. A wrong decision about who needs treatment and who can wait could mean life or death. The feedback on a casualty ward comes thick and fast. On the other hand, a radiologist (a doctor who spends all her time in a darkened room looking at medical images) who makes a mistake can wait months before her diagnosis is confirmed or denied. There is no guarantee she will ever find out.

It is hard to improve, if not impossible, without appropriate, timely feedback. Whose judgement would you trust the most, the triage nurse or the radiologist? This point reinforces the systems thinking three-tiered model we discussed: purpose, interactions, and components. Information flows are one of the interactions between the different parts of an organisation.

Information flows and feedback loops are vital for learning. Yet few managers are happy to pass on information. Avoiding the risk of being criticised for sharing too much is a safer tactic. Who determines the need to know in your organisation? The employee or the manager?

A close relative of the need for secrecy is the careful release of soundbites and single-point data so everybody is on message. Donald Trump was the master of this approach. During his time as president he was not known for his environmental policies.[71] In 2012, he claimed that climate change was "created by and for the

Chinese in order to make US manufacturing non-competitive." He
backed his rhetoric with actions:

- He withdrew from the Paris Climate Agreement in which 195
  countries had committed to keeping the rise in global
  temperatures below 2 degrees Celsius.
- He tried to prevent California from setting its emissions rules
  on motor vehicles.
- He repealed President Obama's Clean Power Plan and
  launched his own Affordable Clean Energy rule, which had far
  weaker regulations.

In true Trump style, he also went on the offensive on Twitter.
One cold day in March, he tweeted: "It's freezing in New York –
Where the hell is global warming?" The soundbites supported his
political beliefs and policies but didn't make him popular with
scientists. The World Meteorological Organisation asserted that
the 20 warmest years on record have been in the past 22 years. No
doubt it was cold in New York that day, but Donald Trump has
never tweeted this chart.[72]

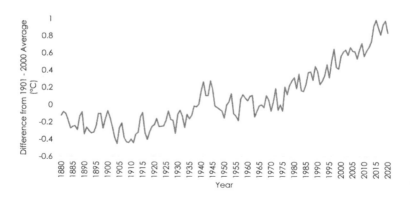

Figure 10: Global Temperature Change

An organisation can't learn or improve if it doesn't realise (or admit) that it has a problem. Information is power, but it is diluted if it isn't shared and acted upon.

Managers Know Best

Chief executives, operations directors and marketing vice presidents didn't start their careers in those elevated roles. Many started as management trainees (read dogsbodies), and some began their careers on the shop floor. They were promoted because of their intelligence, hard work, willingness to get things done and political skill. It is sensible to expect that managers know best, and consequently, workers should do as they are told.

In the 1970s, Ernesto Sirolli worked for an Italian non-governmental organisation (NGO) providing aid in the Republic of Zambia.[73] One of their projects was teaching the Zambians about agriculture and cultivating food. Sirolli tells how they arrived in a beautiful verdant valley on the banks of the river Zambezi. The climate was hot but not dry. The soil was amazingly fertile and a perfect environment for growing beautiful Italian tomatoes and courgettes.

The Italian aid workers quickly set about cultivating the soil and planting their seeds. The locals (who were lazy) had no interest in joining in, so the aid workers started to pay them to help with their endeavours. From time to time, they would show up to collect a wage, but their engagement was, at best, sporadic. As the months passed, the Italians' crops flourished. The tomatoes grew to the size of footballs and the courgettes – that is best left to the imagination. The aid workers were amazed by the fertile valley, and even more shocked that the Africans were not remotely interested in agriculture.

"Thank God we are here", they thought. "We will save the Zambians from starvation."

Just as the plants were ripening a week before it was time to harvest them, a bloat of hippopotamuses emerged from the river and ate everything. It was a disaster. The Italians wailed at the Zambians, "My God, why didn't you tell us about the hippos?" The Africans replied, "You never asked." Was it any wonder they weren't interested in cultivating the valley?

Managers believe they know best, and it is their opinions that count. The reality is different. The more senior the manager, the further they are from the shop floor, and the less they know about the specific operational issues and problems in a business.

The designer Thomas Thwaites reinforced the need to ask the opinions of others when he took it upon himself to try and make a simple electric toaster from scratch.[74] He bought himself the cheapest model he could find (thinking that it would be the easiest to reverse engineer). Yet, to his dismay, when Thwaites started dismantling it, he discovered that the object he had purchased for £3.49 (this was the 2000s) had about 400 components and was made from over 100 different materials. As he says in his subsequent TED Talk, he didn't have the rest of his life to build the toaster, so Thwaites decided to focus on just four materials he would need: steel, mica, copper and plastic.

He started by knocking on the door of the Royal School of Mines, where staff kindly pointed him in the right direction. From there, he visited a disused mine and returned with a suitcase full of iron ore. A visit to the Science Museum's History of Science Library and an online search taught him how to smelt it with a microwave to create iron and then steel.

Another challenge was copper. A retired geology professor showed him how to make enough of the material for a three-pin plug using water collected from the depths of an old copper mine in Anglesey.

Next he collected mica, an excellent electrical insulator, from Scotland. And finally, he tried to make plastic. BP wouldn't let him visit a rig in the North Sea to get a jug full of crude oil, so he had to make do with plant oils and starches. These he cast to make a plastic casing using a mould he had carved from a tree trunk. Unfortunately, after letting it cool in his garden, he returned to find that snails were eating it. Ultimately, he had a brain wave and used recycled plastic to produce an outer insulating shell instead.

After several months he managed to build a complete toaster. Unfortunately, five seconds after he plugged it into the mains, the element melted, and the much-longed-for slice of toast failed to materialise.

The point of Thomas Thwaites' experiment was to show how complex our world has become. Nobody can make a humble toaster from scratch. Individuals have only the faintest understanding of all the technologies, activities, supply chains and markets involved. Imagine the knowledge required to build and operate an aircraft carrier or the trading floor of a bank. It is stored away in the minds of hundreds, if not thousands, of people. Yet surprisingly, senior managers who are far removed from the operational realities, are convinced they are that they have the solution to every problem. They don't appreciate that we live in a very sophisticated and interconnected world.

To learn, an organisation must understand its issues or, as John Boyd would put it, "Observe and Orientate". Managers can only do that by listening to their employees and customers and asking what they think. Managers don't know best – they are too distant from the work. Beware of the HIPPO, the Highest Paid Person's Opinion. Bombastic instructions from senior managers, and the head-long rush to fulfil them, do little for learning or productivity.

Reward Success and Punish Failure

Giving out slaps on the back, public praise, large bonuses and honours to people who have achieved excellent results is easy for us to rationalise. Staff expect their managers to reward them for good performance.

Conventional management wisdom is that if we reward success, people will strive to give us more. Logically that "stands to reason". Yet it isn't that straightforward. If we play a high-stakes game with big bonuses and penalties, then there are downsides:

- People won't try anything new for fear it will go wrong.
- If something starts to fail, people will give up.
- If only success is rewarded, people will never admit to failure.
- If nobody ever tries anything new, perseveres or shares their failures an organisation won't learn.

Praise is a good thing, but high stakes and contingent rewards for success (if you do this, then you will get that) are a recipe for ignorance. As the scientific method shows, people must try new ideas, test them and learn from them. Paradoxically the more they fail, the more they know and the more likely they will succeed. Consequently, you should reward failures and history, or at least the internet will tell you this is true.

> *Anyone who has never made a mistake has never tried anything new.*
>
> *~ Albert Einstein*

> *I've not failed; I've just found ten thousand ways that don't work.*
>
> *~ Thomas Edison*

> *Success is stumbling from failure to failure with no loss*
> *of enthusiasm.*
>
> ~ *Winston Churchill*

Though this point may be intellectually sound, it is emotionally hard to stomach. Failure smells, and rewarding it sticks in managers' craws. The newspapers and politicians would have a field day if they learned that teachers, police officers, surgeons and fire chiefs were rewarded for failure. Few HR managers would recommend a programme that incentivises failure to their chief executives. This reality creates a third paradox, the "Failure Paradox":

Rewarding failure is a fool's errand, yet if people don't fail, the organisation will not succeed.

Fortunately, there is a middle way. Bob Sutton is a professor of management science at Stanford University. He points out that the best predictor of the number of good ideas a person has is the number of ideas he tries. In his book *Weird Ideas that Work,* Sutton suggests that businesses shouldn't reward success or failure, but the number of attempts people make.[75] What counts as an attempt depends on your business, but it could be the number of trials or laboratory experiments undertaken. It could also be the number of prototypes produced, the number of patents registered or the number of test products launched. Sutton argues that businesses should ensure their staff know that the biggest sin isn't failure but inaction.*

Sutton's approach is a pragmatic solution to the problem, but it still violates managers' beliefs. It is a brave supervisor who stands up at an employee's year-end performance rating validation

---

*Sutton's other weird ideas include hiring people who make you feel uncomfortable, even those you dislike as they will make you more creative by forcing you to see the world differently.

session and announces that they are a "good trier". The way managers view success and failure does nothing for learning.

Big and Strategic Beats Small and Tactical

Managers love to be strategic; it demonstrates that they are thinking big. Tactical plays, on the other hand, show a lack of imagination and drive. No manager wants to be labelled that way. For most managers, "big" and "strategic" are synonymous concepts. The more expensive a project is, the more strategic it must be. To build a career, managers must work on big projects and steer clear of anything that sounds inconsequential.

The Big, Career-Enhancing Project

One of the world's most recognisable buildings is located on Bennelong Point on the banks of Sydney Harbour in New South Wales. The Sydney Opera House was designed by the Danish architect Jørn Utzon and opened to the public in 1973.[76] In 2007 it was declared a UNESCO World Heritage site, putting it in the same league as the Taj Mahal, the Acropolis and the Great Pyramids.

Planning for the Opera House began in the late 1940s. The New South Wales Government held an international design competition in 1955, and two years later, after sifting through 233 entries, they awarded the prize to Utzon. Construction work started in 1959, and the government expected the project to take four years and cost seven million Australian dollars (£3.5 million). The opening day was scheduled for the 26th of January (Australia Day), 1963.

However, construction didn't go well as there were several problems that the planners didn't foresee. The government pushed for work to begin before the architect had finished the final designs as they were worried that public opinion would turn against them, and funding would dry up.

By early 1961, the project was already running a year late. The weather was awful, and there had been problems with stormwater. The forced early start and lack of finalised plans resulted in endless rework. The columns weren't strong enough to support the roof structure, and the contractors had to rebuild them. Between 1957 and 1963, the design team went through 12 different iterations of the roof shells (or sails), trying to find an acceptably priced solution. Even the tiles on the roof were problematic. It took a Swedish company three years to develop a solution before the architect was happy.

Fitting out the interior of the building was equally fraught. The contractors only put 2,000 seats in the main hall, which was 1,000 less than the original plan. It transpired that the extra people and seating would have ruined the acoustics. Architects had to change the interior layout, and stage machinery was removed and scrapped, primarily because the initial design brief was inadequate.

As well as the technical challenges, there were political problems to contend with. In 1965, the government of New South Wales changed, and the new government's criticism of progress resulted in the architect's resignation.

Problems continued right the way down the home straight. In 1972, site managers dismissed one of the construction workers, and the building crews went on strike. The project was completed 10 years late and (in real terms) 1,357% over budget.

Big projects invariably take longer, cost more and deliver less than planned. It isn't just the Sydney Opera House that has fallen foul of the phenomenon.[77]

- Planners initially scheduled the Berlin Brandenburg Airport to open in 2011. Commercial traffic started nine years later, in 2020 (during the pandemic).
- A plan to centralise UK patient records was shelved in 2013 after the NHS had spent £10 billion.[78]
- The Scottish Police Authority scrapped its i6 project. The plan was to replace 130 electronic and paper-based systems. Accenture, who was building the system, had to pay £24 million to the police to extricate themselves from the contract.[79]

The reason behind these failures has been christened the "Planning Fallacy".[80] Managers and executives overestimate benefits and underestimate costs in bouts of delusional optimism on nearly every project. These overruns are invariably caused by repeating patterns of management behaviour:

- **Poor personal judgement:** People overestimate their talents. Most of us believe we are better than average drivers, and we also think we are better than average at running large projects.
- **Environmental issues**: We live in a complex world, and a raft of unforeseen problems will delay a project. Unknowns invariably cause the delivery to slide backwards and rarely pull it forward.
- **Organisational politics:** Managers want to look good in front of their bosses, so they overpromise. There are often personal costs for people less than enthusiastic about a large strategic project.

Large, strategically important projects are not the way to learn. Whilst those involved in these projects came away older and wiser, there are easier paths to knowledge.

There are two reasons why big projects aren't good learning vehicles. First, large-scale projects extend the learning loop as they take so long, so it takes an inordinate time to see whether the good idea works. Alternatively, what might have been sensible once becomes embedded in the delivery even though the world has moved on. One of the key points from the OODA loop was speed. It is hard to be responsive at the helm of a multi-million-pound project.

The second issue is cost. If an organisation invests millions in a project, it must be sure it will deliver. So managers only place big project bets against "sure things"; nobody wants to chance failure.

Big projects aren't bad. If the Australian politicians had known the Sydney Opera House would take 10 years longer than planned and be 13 times the cost, they wouldn't have started. There is much to be said for ignorance and bloody-mindedness when used in appropriate quantities. We have a lot to learn from Australian culture. But bloody-mindedness and learning are not the same thing.

Sweating the Small Stuff

In Mumbai, there is an organisation that delivers meals to office workers. It is called the Nutan Mumbai Tiffin Box Suppliers Association.[81] The workers are more commonly known as dabbawalas or lunch box men. Their business model is a little like Deliveroo's, except the meals are delivered from customers' homes, not restaurants.

The dabbawalas started deliveries in the late 19th century when India was under British rule. Thousands of people had migrated to Bombay (as it was then called) looking for a better life. Their offices didn't have canteens, and there was massive variation in ethnic diets, so most people brought packed lunches to work. By lunchtime, these were cold and unappetising. The dabbawalas sprang up to fill a need.[82] They delivered freshly cooked meals from workers' homes in the suburbs to their offices in the city centre. Today, the organisation delivers roughly 200,000 home cooked meals every lunchtime. It employs five thousand people and is claimed to have "Six Sigma" levels of accuracy.* That isn't strictly true, but they are good enough for the rumour to flourish.

The most surprising thing about the Nutan Mumbai Tiffin Box Suppliers Association is that the dabbawalas are a collective of primarily illiterate men (and a few women). They don't have an extensive logistics system or a fleet of vans, and their only sizeable investment is in bicycles. The dabbawalas make all these deliveries without an iPad in sight. What they do have, however, is a finely honed organisation.

First comes purpose. The one the dabbawalas are striving to meet is simple: *"Delivering food on time, every time."* They want to serve their customers punctually. Everything else revolves around that. The dabbawalas take great pride in the job that they do. Mumbai has a diverse cultural mix. Muslims don't eat pork, Jains don't eat onions, potatoes or garlic, and Christians will eat pretty much anything. It could be deeply offensive to deliver the wrong meal. The dabbawalas believe their task is as important as giving medicine to the sick. As they say, "Feeding people is a worthwhile occupation."[83]

The next element is people. The dabbawalas organise themselves into multiple self-managed groups. New members buy their way into the organisation, which costs about ten months' wages. Consequently, there is a tremendous sense of ownership of the business and the service it provides.

Dabbawalas are free to negotiate with their customers. They can also change and adapt their processes to enhance performance.

---

* Six Sigma is a problem-solving method used to reduce errors. If a process has a six sigma level of accuracy, it only produces one defect in every 294,118 opportunities. It is safe to say that the dabbawalas lose more lunch boxes than that. Six Sigma or 6σ (clever marketing) is also beautifully arbitrary. Your processes don't need to be that good unless you make aeroplanes or parts for nuclear power stations, in which case I'd like them to be better.

Yet the dabbawalas have specific rules that they obey. For example, they don't eat until they have completed all their deliveries and never open a tiffin box. In return for this, they earn a reasonable wage for manual work.

Then comes the system. Every morning tiffin boxes are collected from the homes of customers. They are transported by bicycle, cart, rail and hand into the centre of Mumbai. The dabbawalas run a hub and spoke system: each tiffin box (or dabba) can change hands three or four times on its journey. To ensure every box finds its way, they are all coded with marks and numbers. These show the origin and destination of each packet. The dabbawalas learn the code by heart. Once the boxes are delivered, the dabbawalas break for their lunch. They then set about collecting the boxes for the return journey.

The organisation is so reliable that some customers use the returning boxes to transport their wages home. It is safer than carrying the cash personally.

The technology at the heart of the system is Mumbai's ever-punctual rail network. The boxes and the people who carry them use the cargo compartments on each train. The railway system is then extended with baskets, bicycles and carts used for the "last mile" from the station to the office. Where helpful, the groups have invested in more modern tools. You can book a delivery via SMS, and they have a website on which you can place an order, but that is the extent of their information technology.

It is insightful to understand what the system doesn't do. The dabbawalas do not try to be all things to all men – they have absolute clarity of purpose. Customers can't ask for deliveries of unusually shaped dabbas (tins). Uniform shapes and sizes help the dabbawalas to load trains and bicycles efficiently. They expect customers to have the meals ready for pickup at predetermined times. If they are not prepared, the system can flounder. The dabbawalas will drop a customer who is routinely late and expects them to hang around. Some business schools have suggested that the dabbawalas use motorcycles instead of bicycles. That hasn't happened. As one of the senior dabbawalas said, "Then our people would have to learn how to use them, get driver's licences, deal with the Regional Transport Office, and costs would increase for the customer." Besides, bicycles are easier to manoeuvre through narrow lanes and traffic-clogged streets.

The service is simple to describe yet complex to execute. It would be difficult for any other organisation to copy it. It is hard to believe that Uber or FedEx would be able to oust the dabbawalas, no matter how much they invested. The system's power has come from thousands of simple changes developed over the years as the dabbawalas refined their art. They haven't invested in system upgrades or infrastructure projects. Instead, they have worked with what they learned from continuous experimentation and numerous small-scale improvements.

Both big and small projects are vital for businesses. Excellence comes from testing with small-scale experiments that won't destroy the company if they fail and backing them to the hilt whenever they work. But using big projects for organisational learning is like using Scafell Pike to teach my daughter to ride her bicycle. It is an unwise manager who rejects small tests and improvements. Who knows where they could lead?

You Must Be at the Cutting Edge

Management thinking is full of cutting-edge solutions. There is always a deluge of new initiatives that a business's competitors are rolling out, and new tools and technologies are invariably impressive. It is beholden upon managers to ensure that

they are not left behind. Over the past 30 years, businesses have
been busy with:

- Big Data and Analytics
- Customer Journey Mapping
- Customer Relationship Management
- Business Process Re-engineering
- Business Process Outsourcing
- Near Shoring, Off Shoring and On Shoring
- Rapid Process Digitisation and Robotics
- Agile Development
- Total Quality Management
- Big Scale Value Analysis
- Operational Excellence
- Lean
- Six Sigma
- Plus the ones I missed

Every consulting house has its propriety flavour of the above,
which they claim to be infinitely better than anybody else's.
Corporations have spent billions of pounds on cutting-edge
solutions. Unfortunately, these initiatives rarely stick; they result
in "solutioneering" as implementation teams run around looking
for a place to use the sexy new method. Unfortunately, for a
solution to work, managers should understand their problems first
and then look for a solution rather than the other way around.

> *I call it the law of the instrument, and it may be
> formulated as follows: Give a small boy a hammer, and
> he will find that everything he encounters needs
> pounding.*
>
> *~ Abraham Kaplan*

In his TED talk, the advertising guru Rory Sutherland challenged the £6 billion Eurostar spent in the mid-2000s.[84] The money was used to move Eurostar's London terminal from Waterloo to St Pancras and route trains through Stratford and East London. This reduced the travel time from London to Paris by 20 minutes to a fraction over two hours.

> "Why is it necessary to spend six billion pounds speeding up the Eurostar train when, for about 10 per cent of that money, you could have top supermodels, male and female, serving free Chateau Petrus to all the passengers for the entire duration of the journey? You'd still have five billion left in change, and people would ask for the trains to be slowed down."

Though made in jest, Sutherland's point was perfect. It is easy to conclude that journey time was the issue that Eurostar had to solve. That was what necessitated such a considerable capital investment, but Sutherland argues that the problem was passenger boredom.

It is easier and more politically acceptable for a manager to explain poor performance by the lack of investment in up-to-date thinking and technology rather than taking the time to define their problems and test solutions. Managers don't need to be at the cutting edge, but they do need to understand and articulate their problems. Regard anybody who says "the problem is we don't have [insert favoured solution here]" with the most profound suspicion.

The Action is at Head Office

Organisations are hierarchical. Careers are made at corporate headquarters with the movers and shakers, not on their fringes in minor branch offices, factories and customer service centres. A manager can do the best job in the world in the provinces, but if nobody sees him, he wastes his time. This attitude is often combined with the beliefs that "Information is Power", "Managers Know Best", and the reality that the corporate outposts are a long and uncomfortable journey away. So, it is easy to understand why managers huddle around the corporate centre. It is career suicide to spend your working life at the operational fringes of an organisation, yet often, that is where the answers are.

Short Breaks Will Kill You: A Management Fable

A statistician who worked for a large organisation was asked to explain why sick pay was increasing. The statistician went about his work, gathering data on lots of things:

- *Working patterns*
- *Demographics*
- *Employment related illnesses*
- *Commuting times*
- *Office locations…*

The list went on. Like all good statisticians, he liked numbers. Once he had the data, he started to analyse it, looking for patterns and extracting the signal from the noise. He ran single-factor investigations, multivariate regressions, random forests and clustering algorithms. If he had the data and the computing power, he ran the analysis, leaving no stone unturned.

Eventually, he came across a startling relationship. The more breaks an employee had during the day, the more likely they were to be sick and have long periods off work later in their career. The statistics were compelling, but entirely against the conventional wisdom his colleagues in HR expounded. They were sure that regular short breaks reduced stress and increased productivity.

The statistician produced graphs, he presented PowerPoint packs and he enlisted executive sponsorship. He was unstoppable. HR wrote a new policy and prepared it for launch. Managers would minimise work breaks during the day. It was a win-win. Not only would this enhance productivity, but it would also improve employee health and wellness.

The organisation was about to launch the new policy when an occupational nurse pointed out a minor flaw in the analysis. She had spent her career talking to sick staff members and was convinced that short breaks were good for concentration and well-being unless you used them to nip outside for a smoke.

The breaks weren't making staff sick. The cigarettes were.

There are two types of analysis. Quantitative analysis is the approach beloved by numerate analysts and management consultants. It is hard and fact-based, requires lots of data and identifies the right direction. Quantitative analysis can also be done from the safety of a head office. Unfortunately, quantitative analysis is wide and shallow. It shows where to look but doesn't explain what is going on.

By contrast, qualitative analysis is beloved by humanities students and people who wear brown sandals. It is soft and observation based. To conduct a qualitative study, researchers must leave the comfort of their offices, talk to people and watch what they do. Qualitative research is expensive and takes time. It is easy to dismiss because it isn't statistically valid, and doesn't show anything like the whole picture. Qualitative analysis is deep but narrow, however it is the best way to understand what is happening, assuming it is directed at the right place.

Quantitative analysis shows the relationship between short breaks and sickness. Qualitative research proves that cigarettes, not breaks, are bad for the workforce.

It isn't possible to see how an organisation works if the view is only taken from the boardroom in corporate headquarters staring at reports and presentations. In the late 1990s the BBC made 36 episodes of a programme, *Back to the Floor*, in which senior managers took on junior jobs in their companies. The series spanned diverse industries, from His Majesty's Prisons to Butlin's Holiday Camps. The programme proved the point 36 times: the senior managers didn't understand the struggles their employees faced.

Managers must go and look. Neither customers nor enlightenment is to be found at head office.

> *A desk is a dangerous place from which to watch the world.*
>
> ~ *John le Carré*

Problems Are a Sign of Weakness

Good managers shouldn't have problems; they are paid to solve them. Competent managers address issues and understand what is happening in their area. Admitting to their boss that there is a problem is abhorrent to a professional manager.

The Americans have an unpleasant phrase – to "fess-up" or confess. It means you acknowledge your issue and take responsibility for it. It isn't a nice thing to do, but it can be a potent approach in the right environment.

When Alan Mulally became chief executive of the failing Ford Motor Company in 2006, he introduced a "traffic light" system at his weekly staff meetings.[85] Mulally asked his executives to report progress as red, amber, or green. For the next four weeks, Mulally saw a sea of green. Eventually, Mulally became frustrated and challenged his team. "Well, that's interesting. We lost $10 billion last year, but everybody's green. How does that work?" His question was met with silence. Ford had a culture where managers never talked about problems; it was seen as a sign of weakness. There was a crippling fear of discussing issues without an immediate solution. Executives were not prepared to fess-up.

A week later, Ford's North American President, Mark Fields, produced a red report because a factory he oversaw had gone offline.[86] The other executives around the table assumed Mulally would flip and that this would end Fields' career. But Mulally applauded him and asked the rest of the group what they could do to help. Another executive admitted they had a similar problem, and a third offered a potential solution. It took a while, but the weekly staff meetings became a rainbow of red, amber and green.

In the same way, Alcoholics Anonymous encourages its members to admit they are alcoholics. If you aren't prepared to accept that you have a problem, you will never fix it. One of the most significant barriers to improving productivity is an inability to fess-up.

> *You have a problem; you are not the problem.*
>
> *~ Alan Mulally*

When Mulally took over the top job at Ford in 2006, the company expected to lose $17 billion. When he left in 2014, his successor inherited a company making $7.2 billion.[87]

The issue at Ford and many other companies is that managers are horrified by admitting they have a problem they don't know how to solve. They regard ignorance as failure. If a manager doesn't know what to do, there is invariably somebody younger, brighter and hungrier who is happy to take their place.

Consequently, managers believe they must always show that they are on their A-game and know everything there is to know about their business. The perversity of this is that no manager can hope to know everything (remember the complexity of the toaster?)

Problems aren't a sign of weakness, but pretending you don't have any most definitely is. Managers who claim to be all-knowledgeable force themselves into exposed places. Donald Rumsfeld, then US Secretary of Defence, was wise to this when, in 2002, he held a press conference about weapons of mass destruction in Iraq and admitted that he didn't know everything.

> "…there are known knowns; there are things we know we know. We also know there are known unknowns; that is to say, we know there are some things we do not know. But there are also unknown unknowns — the ones we don't know we don't know."

He highlighted that knowledge can be classified in four ways:

- **Known knowns:** The things you know that you know. I know I know the way to my front door, and I know the names of my wife and daughters. This is a safe place to be.
- **Unknown knowns:** The things you don't know that you know. I know the lyrics to many 1980s pop songs, though I couldn't tell you which. I only know when I hear one played on the radio. This is a safe but unnerving place to be.
- **Known unknowns:** The things you know that you don't know. I know I don't know any Chinese. This is also a safe place to be. I will have the sense to download a phrasebook if I ever go to Beijing.
- **Unknown unknowns:** The things you don't know that you don't know. It is hard to pinpoint this area of knowledge. You feel confident that you know something, and that confidence is

unshakeable, but that confidence is misplaced and your enemy. Occasionally, while driving in Europe, I have caught myself driving on the left-hand side of the road. I thought I knew which side of the road to drive on and everything was OK, and then suddenly, it wasn't. The stuff that you don't know you don't know can be deadly. This is a dangerous place to be.

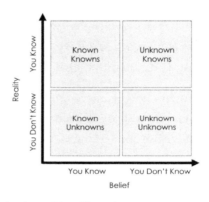

Figure 11: Knowledge Classification

All of which leads to a couple of interesting observations. The first is the surprising revelation that the absolute safest place to be is knowing you don't know. Known ignorance is a position of total strength. You cannot be surprised. The second is more worrying. To look good in front of the boss, we often claim to know something we don't. That is foolish, we could get caught out, but it gets worse as we start to believe our own press. Then we deliberately put ourselves in a position of not knowing what we don't know, the most dangerous place of all.

> *It ain't what you don't know that gets you into trouble;*
> *it's what you know for sure that just ain't so.*
>
> *~ Mark Twain*

Whenever a manager isn't prepared to admit there is a problem or claims to know the solution when he doesn't, he shuts down the opportunities to learn. Why run an experiment if you haven't got a problem, or already know the answer? This last management belief, that problems are a sign of weakness, is the largest barrier to learning. Taiichi Ohno was a Japanese industrial engineer and an executive at Toyota. His most famous quote sums up how dangerous this management attitude can be.

> *Having no problems is the biggest problem of all.*
>
> *~ Taiichi Ohno*

Summary

Key Points

There are (at least) seven management beliefs or conceits that prevent learning. They are:

- Belief 1: Information is power.
- Belief 2: Managers know best.
- Belief 3: You should reward success and punish failure.
- Belief 4: Big and strategic beats small and tactical.
- Belief 5: You must be at the cutting edge.
- Belief 6: The action is at head office.
- Belief 7: Problems are a sign of weakness.

These beliefs are related and overlap. They create dysfunctional behaviours when it becomes more pressing that the manager looks good than learns or grows. They prevent experimentation and stop the testing and learning cycle.

Actions

Challenge yourself: which of these beliefs do you hold? Ask your staff if they see any negative behaviours because of these beliefs. Pick one belief and try to break it. What happens if you:

- Share honest performance information with your teams.
- Ask employees their opinions.
- Reward trials rather than success.
- Start testing and learning.
- Reinforce the best of the last "cutting-edge" initiative rather than giving lip service to the next.
- Leave your office and visit the outposts.
- Admit you have a problem and ask for help.

Chapter 8:
Remember Your Lessons

Learning From Disasters, Some Far Worse than Others

Every time an organisation learns and builds capability, it becomes more productive. But there is no point in learning something if is promptly ignored or forgotten.

The Forgetful Organisation

At approximately 5pm on Monday, the 22nd of June 2009, a Washington Metro train heading towards Shady Grove collided with a stationary train on the track ahead of it.[88] The Automatic Train Control (ATC) system had instructed the train to pull out of a station and accelerate to full speed (55 miles per hour). When the driver of the moving train, Jeanice McMillan, saw the carriages ahead, she applied the emergency brakes, but it was too late to avoid a crash.

Within 20 minutes, rescuers arrived on the scene. The front compartment of the moving train had climbed over the stationary carriage ahead of it, and the two trains had slid together like a closing telescope, trapping many passengers. Survivors said the crash was "like… hit[ting] a concrete wall."[89] The air was full of smoke and debris, and passengers panicked when the train doors didn't open. Ultimately, there were over 200 firefighters at the scene. They worked throughout the night, and had to use cranes to free trapped passengers and search for bodies. Jeanice McMillan and eight other people died. At least 80 were injured. The death toll made it the most severe crash the Metro has ever had.

The National Transportation Safety Board began an inquiry. Investigators considered several possible causes. They looked at operator error, brake failure, a fault in the ATC and countless other factors. They confirmed that the moving rear train had been running under the guidance of the ATC. The driver had used the emergency brake when the automation failed to stop it. The breakthrough in understanding came when the investigators showed that the track signalling system below the stationary front train wasn't working. It had failed to detect the stationary train's presence; as far as the ATC was concerned, the front train wasn't there. According to Deborah Hersman, Chair of the National Transportation Safety Board, a critical part of the control infrastructure wasn't working. "These circuits are vital. It's a signal system. It's providing information, authorisation, and speed commands to the following train."

The Washington Metro has a sophisticated track signalling mechanism. It allows the ATC, drivers and central controllers to see whether there is a train on any section of the track. An electric current flows along one rail between two sensors. If there isn't a train on that section, the current passes unhindered, and the controllers know that the rails are empty. If, however, there is a train, the current doesn't make it from one sensor to the next. Instead, it skips across the metal train wheels and axles to the other track and shorts out to earth.

It is a clever system, but as with all things, there is wear and tear, parts age and the machinery needs regular maintenance. The primary cause of the accident was that the ATC didn't "see" the train that had stopped and let the second train keep on running.

Maintenance engineers had discovered this problem four years earlier, in 2005, after a series of near misses in the tunnel between

Foggy Bottom and Rosslyn stations. It was a known issue. To stop a reoccurrence, they designed a preventative maintenance check. During the night and weekends when rail traffic was light, teams of workers should have walked down the tracks with a metal bar and laid it across the two rails at every section to mimic the trains' wheels and axles. Using this check, they would have ensured that the system was working and that they didn't need to replace or repair anything.

Safety engineers understood the problem, but the maintenance crews were not completing the checks. The rail operator had failed to institutionalise the knowledge.[90] An engineering bulletin and safety notice had been issued, but the check wasn't well documented, managers hadn't trained the staff and there wasn't any reinforcement. The maintenance crews on the Shady Grove section of the line weren't aware of the safety protocol.

The National Transportation Safety Board cited the Washington Metro's lack of a safety culture and failure to monitor and maintain its ATC system as contributing causes of the accident. The organisation had forgotten what it had learnt.

Our organisations are vast, and it is easy to miss or forget issues, but it doesn't have to be that way. On the 15th of January 2009, US Airways flight 1549 struck a flock of geese as it climbed away from New York City's LaGuardia Airport.[91] The plane lost all engine power. The pilots, Chesley Sullenberger and Jeffrey Skiles, were forced to land on the River Hudson off Midtown Manhattan. Boats rescued all 155 passengers and crew. Only five people were seriously injured. An official from the National Transportation Safety Board described the event as "the most successful ditching in aviation history."

The chief pilot, Chesley Sullenberger, was showered with honours. President-elect Obama said he was proud of

Sullenberger's "heroic and graceful job in landing the damaged aircraft." The media also depicted Chesley Sullenberger as a hero, and I certainly wouldn't have kept my nerve in such a situation. But (according to Matthew Syed in his book, *Black Box Thinking*) in a television interview given months after the event, Sullenberger was sage enough to say:[92]

> "Everything we know in aviation, every rule in the rule book, every procedure we have, we know because someone somewhere died..."

> "We have purchased, at great cost, lessons literally bought with blood that we have to preserve as institutional knowledge and pass on to succeeding generations. We cannot have the moral failure of forgetting these lessons and have to relearn them."

The lesson from the Washington Metro tragedy is that it isn't enough to write up a report after an incident detailing the measures you have put in place to stop it from happening again. You must have a system that ensures those checks and controls are applied and maintained, not abandoned or neglected. Fortunately, as Chesley Sullenberger insisted, there are many ways an organisation can remember what it has learnt.

Four Ways to Fix a Problem

Imagine you come across a homeless person who is hungry and begging for food. There are four ways you could solve his problem and take away his hunger:

1. Insult him and kick him. If you create enough pain and confusion, you will distract him, and the problem will disappear.
2. Give him a fish to eat. That will satiate his hunger.

3.   Give him a fishing rod and show him how to fish.
4.   Develop a first-world infrastructure with trawlers, freezers, distribution centres, corner stores and fish fingers.

I'd love to claim credit for this line of thinking, but it came from Russell L. Ackoff.[93] He called the four methods "absolve, resolve, solve and dissolve". His point was that the further we take our problem-solving and embed the learning, the more likely we will make the pain disappear forever.

> *We never have time to fix anything, yet we always have time to fix it twice.*
>
> *~ Anon*

Problem Absolution or Lazy Thinking

The root cause of any business problem can invariably be tracked down to human error. Somebody always messed up something. That person either forgot to do something, did it incorrectly, or designed a solution poorly. If you ask "Why?" often enough, you will ultimately find that a human screwed up. Human error is rife. The most common management approach to prevent human error is:

- **Step 1:** Find the human. Point out the error of their ways and train them so they do not repeat the error. If this doesn't work, then move on to step 2.
- **Step 2:** Hold the human accountable for the error and sack them. Then find a new (presumably better) human who won't make the same error.

Step 1, training, is always helpful. But training isn't something you can depend on. Sooner or later, human error will rear its head again. It is far better to improve the system. Step 2 just absolves the manager of all obligations. Whilst they have "taken firm action", it doesn't fix the problem.

Managers believe their role is "people management" and ensuring their staff don't make mistakes. However, expecting perfection and blaming your team when things go wrong doesn't change the system and won't stop the problem from reoccurring, no matter how much weight managers throw about. It is lazy thinking to assume it will.

The Cleverest People Make Mistakes

On Sunday, the 26th of February 2017, The Academy of Motion Picture Arts and Sciences held its 89th award ceremony, celebrating the previous year's best films. The ceremony is a case study in human error. It went swimmingly until the very last award for best picture.[94]

Faye Dunaway and Warren Beatty mounted the stage. They read the nominees aloud, and then Warren Beatty opened the envelope containing the winner's name. Beatty looked a bit puzzled. He checked the inside of the envelope to ensure he wasn't missing something and gave Faye Dunaway a quizzical look, then started to announce the award and stopped. With a bemused expression, he looked inside the envelope again.

Mr Beatty passed the card to Faye Dunaway to see what she made of it. Thinking he was clowning about and not genuinely confused, Ms Dunaway shouted out the winner: "La La Land".

Two minutes later, halfway through the acceptance speeches, all hell broke loose. Stage managers and organisers crowded onto the platform. Faye Dunaway had read out the wrong card. La La Land's producer Jordan Horowitz rectified the error when he said,

"I'm sorry, no, there has been a mistake. Moonlight, you guys won best picture."

Jimmy Kimmel, the show's host, regained control of the situation and asked in mock outrage, "What did you do, Warren?" It was easy to blame Warren Beatty – after all, he was the first to realise that the card was wrong. He should never have shown it to Faye Dunaway, but what was he supposed to do? As he pointed out later, the show must go on. In an interview, he explained his thought process, "Well, maybe this is a misprint... I shouldn't foul up the show just because someone made a little error."[95]

It wasn't Beatty's fault. Somebody had given him the wrong card. One of the people handing out the results envelopes that evening was Brian Cullinan, a partner at PricewaterhouseCoopers (PwC), one of the world's largest firms of accountants. PwC is responsible for running the secret ballot for the awards. They pass the result to the announcer at the very last moment so that it remains a secret. Mr Cullinan inadvertently gave Warren Beatty the wrong card and, in so doing, created a public relations disaster for PwC.

Fortunately, nobody was hurt in this calamity. Some of us experienced a lovely dose of schadenfreude watching the beautiful people looking stupid. Yet despite that, when things go wrong, the management rules are simple (if misguided). First, find the operator who made the error and second, remove the operator. In this case, Brian Cullinan screwed up. Nobody else was to blame, and Mr Cullinan was held accountable for the issue. It was a clear-cut case of human error.

While diagnosing a fault as human error is easy, it won't prevent the problem from happening again because blaming the human ignores the system within which the human works. A better line of reasoning would be to ask what was wrong with the system. How did the operator make such a foolish error? He was, after all, a highly paid and well-educated partner with PwC, not a minimum-wage worker that had been dragged off the street.

There were (at least) three systems failures that contributed to the show-biz catastrophe. The primary reason why Brian Cullinan messed up was that he was distracted and playing on his mobile phone. Seconds before handing over the wrong envelope, he had taken a picture of Emma Stone and posted it on Twitter. She had just received the award for best actress.[96]

If ever there was evidence that you should "put your damn phone down", this was it. Yet, it is human nature to play with your phone. Arguably Apple designed the iPhone with that single outcome in mind. Mr Cullinan was having the time of his life. One of the world's most beautiful women had walked straight past him, and he took a quick snap and then posted his bragging rights online. How many other men would have done the same? His behaviour was hardly surprising.

The second system failure was the design of the card. When Warren Beatty read the card in his hand, it made him pause for thought. It looked like the card for the last prize, but he wasn't sure. Faye Dunaway had no doubts when she glanced at it and mistakenly read aloud the winner.

The piece of information to which the design gave the most weight was "The Oscars". That was the least helpful thing on the card. The presenters knew that they were at the Oscars. Next most prominent, in equal weight, were the names of the actress and film. Which was most important? In this case, the card was for the best actress. The film's title was secondary. Finally, the designer had tucked away the award's name in the small print at the bottom. Like everybody else, Warren Beatty doesn't read the small print.

With this insight, it is pretty easy to understand why Mr Beatty looked confused and why Ms Dunaway (in the heat of the moment) couldn't help but shout out the name of the only film on the card.

Figure 12: Oscar Award Card

The designer Benjamin Bannister proposed an alternative design that was far clearer.[97] If the card had followed Bannister's design, the presenters would have been far more likely to pause. After all, a minute's delay would have saved everybody's blushes.

Figure 13: Revised Award Card

That isn't the end of the story. The envelope on which the name of the award was written was red with gold lettering. Gold on red is a very opulent look, but it is not hugely legible. The envelopes had been printed to add style to the event; the printers called them "couture envelopes".[98] Warren Beatty was days away from turning 80 when Brian Cullinan handed him that envelope. I'm 54 and struggle to read without my glasses. I imagine Mr Beatty suffers similarly. The whole design was a triumph of style over substance. If you present information ambiguously, somebody will misunderstand it. It doesn't matter if it is on an award card, a PowerPoint or the control panel of a nuclear power station – clarity matters.

Ten minutes earlier, Leonardo DiCaprio had presented the best actress award to Emma Stone. He had already opened the envelope and read the result. This fact begs the question; how did the card find its way back into the hands of Warren Beatty? This duplication was the third system failure. It transpires that there were two identical sets of envelopes. Another partner at PwC, Martha Ruiz, had handed Leonardo DiCaprio one of the Best Actress envelopes earlier, leaving the other in Mr Cullinan's hands. In an interview given before the awards, Brian Cullinan explained why they had two sets of cards.[99]

> "From a security perspective, we double up everything. That's why there's two of us. We have two briefcases that are identical, and we have two entire sets of winning envelopes. Martha carries one of those briefcases; I carry the other. The security is obviously intense because you know, we are literally holding a briefcase filled with secrets.

> We go to the show separately with police escorts. I used to think it was for our security; it's really for the briefcase. We take different routes to get there just because of the kinds of things that can happen in LA traffic. We want to make sure that no matter what happens, one of us gets there. We've never really had a problem with that."

The reason why there were two sets of envelopes was, bizarrely, a safety measure. Yet by adding more controls, the operation became more complicated, so rather than making things safer, the organisers had introduced a new way for things to go wrong.

Who was to blame? There are several scapegoats I could name:

- **Faye Dunaway** blurted out the answer without reading the card.
- **Warren Beatty** gave her what he thought was incorrect information.
- **Brian Cullinan** passed the wrong card to Mr Beatty.
- **The stage manager** didn't insist that Mr Cullinan put down his phone.
- **The designer** created unclear cards and envelopes.
- **The risk manager** decided that there should be two sets of envelopes.

If any of them had made a different decision, the fiasco could have been avoided. Mistakes rarely happen when one thing goes wrong. A string of errors caused the Oscar debacle.

> *The search for a scapegoat is the easiest of all hunting expeditions.*
>
> *~ Dwight D. Eisenhower*

After owning up to the mistake and apologising to all concerned, PwC managed to keep the contract to run the secret ballot. Vanity Fair detailed the extra measures that PwC put in place to prevent future human errors and ensure no further mishaps.[100]

- Brian Cullinan was banned from handing out other awards.

- Cullinan's partner that evening, Martha Ruiz, was also told her services were no longer required.
- The PwC partners who replaced Cullinan and Ruiz memorise the award winners before the event.
- As each envelope is handed out, the accountants, presenters and a stage manager check that it is correct.
- A third PwC partner is backstage with an additional set of envelopes. Senior Partner at PwC, Tim Ryan, described this as "a safety control".[101]

PwC obeyed the golden rules of finding the operator who made the error and removing him. Brian Cullinan undoubtedly failed, but I suspect he learned from the experience. He is probably the only man in the world who can be relied on not to make the same mistake again. Martha Ruiz (who, as far as I can tell, was blameless) would undoubtedly have given him a more than stiff pep talk to keep him in line. PwC has discounted this hard-won knowledge. Instead, they continue to rely on fallible humans (to memorise results and carry out manual inspections) and have thrown another set of cards into the mix. Just in case.

Personally, I'm sceptical that these actions mitigate the risk of future mishaps. Fortunately, these "improvements" have only been applied to the Academy Awards, not something more critical like a fire station or nuclear submarine. On a much more positive note, the Academy has forbidden PwC partners from using mobile phones during the show and changed the design of its cards and envelopes to something far less ambiguous.

Whilst nobody was hurt during the Oscar debacle, pointing at human error as the root cause of the problem can have far more severe consequences. Bomber pilots, as well as accountants, make mistakes.

Over 70 million people were killed during the Second World War. That amounted to roughly 3% of the worldwide population. It was a hazardous time to be alive. Amongst the most brutally hit were the air force bomber crews. The Eighth Air Force suffered half of all the US Air Force's casualties.[102] The British fared as badly.[103] The chances of surviving the war as a member of the Royal Air Force (RAF) bomber command were worse than one in two.

If bombing raids weren't tricky enough, landing when returning home was also fraught with danger. Pilots of the Boeing B-17 Flying Fortress had a series of runway crashes, accidentally retracting the landing gear just as they touched down.[104] Accident investigators blamed these incidents on pilot (or human) error, as there was no apparent mechanical failure. It wasn't only Flying Fortresses that crashed on their return home. There were incidents of pilots of P-47 Thunderbolts and B-25 Mitchells making precisely the same mistake.

The worst thing about this was that it was a schoolboy error. Nobody would deliberately retract the landing gear when hurtling across the tarmac. Why the pilots did this was anybody's guess. The only reason investigators could give was that they were so relieved to be back home, safe and sound, that their attention wandered.

The authorities asked Alphonse Chapanis, a military psychologist, to explain the behaviour. He noticed that the crashes only happened to certain planes and not others (in the same way that John Snow saw that cholera deaths only occurred on some streets). Thousands of C-47 transport planes were buzzing about, yet their pilots never suffered from such fatal inattention. After inspecting the cockpits of the different planes, the cause became apparent. On B-17s, the controls for the flaps and undercarriage were next to one another. They also had the same style of handle.

Pilots who raised the undercarriage when the wheels were on the ground were trying to retract the flaps. They just pulled the wrong lever. In the C-47, the two controls were very different and positioned apart, so the crashes didn't happen on those planes.

Once he identified the cause of the crashes, Chapanis developed an equally simple solution. He stuck circular rubber disks to the levers for the undercarriage and attached triangles to the levers for the flaps (giving pilots a clear and easily remembered cue). When pilots touched the rubber, they felt the difference, and the crashes stopped. By improving the design of the levers, Chapanis helped ensure the air force remembered what he had learnt. He started to dissolve the problem.*

To err is human. Brian Cullinan didn't intentionally hand out the wrong Oscar award card, and the pilots of the second world war planes knew they shouldn't raise the landing gear whilst on the ground. It was "human error" that caused the mistake. But laying the blame on the pilots (or the accountants) will never remove the error. We all make mistakes. It is in our nature.

Most management practice focuses on managing people to prevent errors. We blame people, train people, incentivise people, quality check people, replace people and add more people. Yet none of this will overcome the underlying problem that people make mistakes. Whilst it is easy to point out that the root cause of most problems is human error, it is hard (if not impossible) to fix the human. Changing responsibilities and asking somebody else to do a task is no guarantee that the new person won't make precisely the same mistake.

Managing individuals and "holding them accountable" is how managers absolve themselves from responsibility ("It wasn't me; it was them"). A better alternative is implementing solutions that

---

* Chapanis coined the term "design error" rather than use the phrase "pilot error" to explain the issue.

start to dissolve the problem, building capability with a progressively more sophisticated and clever system design that bakes learning in.

Resolving and Solving Problems

Absolving problems doesn't fix them; it distracts attention away from them. Resolving a problem (giving the man a fish) is little better as it only solves problems temporarily. The management equivalent is to throw resources at an issue. It will fix the symptom but not the cause. When the money runs out and those additional staff and resources are removed, the problem will return.

Though valid, solving a problem (the fishing rod) involves current knowledge. A problem with a known solution should have been fixed already. Known solutions should be rolled out as far and fast as possible (as the Washington Metro tragedy showed), not left until a problem reasserts itself. When I was a graduate trainee, one of my first bosses pointed out rather acidly, "We should know what the business knows." There is little point in reinventing the wheel.

The only worthwhile use of managers' (or paid problem solvers') time is dissolving problems by building an ever-improving infrastructure of solutions and controls. Dissolving problems is the activity that drives all progress. If you haven't spent time today learning and building a more robust solution than the one you had yesterday, then you haven't progressed.

Dissolving Problems

Our default setting when trying to remove problems is to build a technological solution and invest in machines or computers. Or better still, robots, which are the best of both worlds.

For example, robotic surgery equipment is big news in the medical world. Hospitals are installing robots in operating theatres across the western hemisphere. The robots allow surgeons to make smaller incisions and work much more precisely. The surgeon doesn't have to contend with slippery instruments, and the robot has a steadier hand. The technology helps surgeons perform minimally invasive or keyhole surgery. This investment is good news for patients and medical staff.[105] The technology's advantages include shorter hospital stays, less pain post-operation, a reduction in the amount of blood transfused and a faster recovery. Another advantage of the technology is that the surgeon can operate the robot remotely. He could be anywhere in the world, provided he has a data connection. This versatility means patients can visit their local hospital without travelling to the surgeon or waiting for him to visit.

Since 2000, surgeons have performed more than five million robot-assisted procedures. This begs the question, why wouldn't you want a robot surgeon? The company Intuitive (makers of the da Vinci surgical robot) point out in their sales literature:

"…technology should enhance your ability and help you make better-informed decisions. Da Vinci® systems give you precision, flexibility, and control to perform many types of procedures, while offering real-time feedback so you can operate with confidence…"

Even though they are a cutting-edge, strategic response to surgical problems, robots are not the solution to all operating woes:

• Robots are expensive; they can cost up to $2.5 million.

- Surgeons need to relearn their craft, as using a robot differs from doing the job by hand. It can take 250 procedures to learn how to use a robot.
- Robots can only be used for specific procedures.
- There is limited evidence that the clinical outcomes are any better than surgery performed by a human.[106]

I am not a Luddite. There is a role for robotics in nearly every profession (medicine, the law, insurance, banking, farming), but as a way of improving performance, robotics is not yet a slam-dunk success. There are alternative, far more low-tech ways to enhance surgical performance.

Dull but Useful

In his book, *The Checklist Manifesto*, surgeon Atul Gawande puts forward the case for a far simpler solution than robots: the humble checklist.[107] Despite their use by many other professions, according to Gawande, there is a reluctance to embrace checklists in medicine. Some doctors see them as dumbing down and a failure of skilled professionals to be able to memorise simple tasks. They argue that years of studying and clinical training negate their use. They also contend that in an emergency, checklists are simply a hindrance. They slow the action down. Some doctors believe they are immune to human error.

Yet the low-tech solution works. A study by the World Health Organisation (WHO) looked at the use of checklists in "safe surgery" across various procedures and countries. They tested a simple checklist that called out tasks that medical staff should complete at three critical stages during any surgical procedure: just before anaesthesia, before skin incision and finally before leaving the operating theatre.

The results were impressive. The rate of post-surgery medical complications dropped from 11.0% to 7.0%, and the in-hospital death rate almost halved from 1.5% to 0.8%.[108] The overall rates of surgical-site infection and unplanned reoperation also declined significantly.

It is a sad reflection on human nature that robots impress us, and we give the humble checklist the cold shoulder. Creating a well-designed checklist, whatever your problem, is a very effective (and cheap) way of maintaining knowledge. Robots are, however, sexier.

Whilst checklists may be valuable, if they are ignored, they are pointless. The next level of sophistication is a checklist to check that the checklists have been used. This is the sort of solution that is beloved of clipboard monkeys the world over, but if a checklist is dull, a checklist for checklists is positively tedious. If done well, though, it can be very rock and roll.

Pop stars have a reputation for antisocial antics and bad behaviour, but for real immaturity, you need to look at the world of Heavy Metal. For example, take the story of Van Halen and the brown M&M's. In typical self-aggrandising style, Van Halen wrote a rider into their contract whenever they went on tour. It stated they should always have fruit, coffee and "munchies" (their word, not mine) available. The munchies should include a bowl of M&M's with all the brown ones removed. This is apparently what multi-millionaire rock stars do to make their presence felt – it is as if they don't appreciate that people have better things to do with their time than fish about for brown sweets. On one occasion in Pueblo, Colorado, the band's lead singer, David Lee Roth, found some brown M&M's in the bowl. He lost his temper and allegedly caused $85,000 worth of damage to the arena where they were due to perform.

There is a little more to the tale than I have alluded to. Van Halen was among the first groups to take "mega concerts" (again, their term, not mine) to small, second and third-level concert venues. David Lee Roth tells the story in his autobiography.[109]

The Brown M&M's

"We'd pull up with nine eighteen-wheeler trucks, full of gear, where the standard was three trucks, max. And there were many, many technical errors — whether it was the girders couldn't support the weight, or the flooring would sink in, or the doors weren't big enough to move the gear through.

The contract rider read like a version of the Chinese Yellow Pages because there was so much equipment, and so many human beings to make it function. So just as a little test, in the technical aspect of the rider, it would say 'Article 148: There will be fifteen amperage voltage sockets at twenty-foot spaces, evenly, providing nineteen amperes …' This kind of thing. And article number 126, in the middle of nowhere, was: 'There will be no brown M&M's in the backstage area, upon pain of forfeiture of the show, with full compensation.'

So, when I would walk backstage, if I saw a brown M&M in that bowl … well, line-check the entire production. Guaranteed you're going to arrive at a technical error. They didn't read the contract. Guaranteed you'd run into a problem. Sometimes it would threaten to just destroy the whole show. Something like, literally, life-threatening."

The brown M&M's signalled that the crew hadn't followed the checklist. As for the $85,000 damage in Pueblo, Mr Roth's antics caused roughly $5,000. The staging, sound and lighting equipment that the band brought with them caused the other $80,000. It was so heavy that it sank through the basketball arena's floor. Mr

Roth's behaviour may have been questionable, but the promoter hadn't read the contract. The M&M's were a visual fail-safe check in the document. They were the band's way of checking that the promoter had read the checklist.

Easy to Get Right, Hard to Get Wrong

An alternative method to checklists is to design equipment, software and processes so that they are easy for the user to get right and hard to get wrong.

One of the potential hazards of being a gentleman in the modern world is "splash-back". When we visit a urinal, the urine stream may hit the porcelain and bounce back. This mishap can cause anguish, unpleasant odours and a pool of something nasty on the floor. Splash-back is particularly distressing for those of us who wear light-coloured trousers.

A group of engineers found a solution to the problem. They altered the urinal's curvature to minimise the likelihood of spillage. This design was brilliant engineering, but there was a flaw. There is a sweet spot on the urinal wall where the fluid dynamics are most effective. As the sweet spot isn't apparent, and men aren't known for their attention to detail, the problem remained. A Dutch maintenance engineer at Schiphol Airport, Jos van Bedoff, addressed the design flaw by drawing a fly on the sweet spot. Every male is, at heart, still a boy, and to a man, we instinctively aim at the fly to give it a good drenching. The increased accuracy not only prevents splash-back, but is also claimed to reduce spillage by 80%.[110] (How this was measured, I can't begin to contemplate.)

Design solutions are a powerful mechanism for promoting and locking in learning. Those design solutions can work in two ways. Like the Schiphol fly, they can make it easy for people to do the right thing. They can also make it hard to do something wrong.

From the start of the industrial revolution to the mid-20th century, the British used coal gas as an energy source. It lit streets, fired boilers and cooked roast dinners. Coal gas was a by-product of the coke manufacturing industry. Heating coal without oxygen removes the impurities and produces coke, which can be mixed with iron to make steel. The manufacturers collected the unwanted contaminants and made coal gas, which can be burnt as fuel. During the Victorian, Edwardian and early New Elizabethan years, coal gas was used extensively throughout the UK.

That changed in the 1960s when geologists discovered natural gas in the North Sea. Natural gas was cheaper, cleaner and easier to produce than coal gas. So much so that during the sixties and seventies, the UK Gas Board spent hundreds of millions of pounds switching the supply away from coal gas. Millions of domestic, commercial and industrial customers converted their equipment (boilers, ovens, heaters and generators) to natural gas.

Coincidentally, during the same period as the gas conversion, suicide rates dropped substantially in the UK.[111]

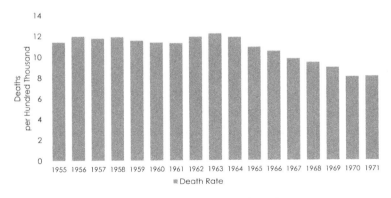

Figure 14: Suicide Rates in England and Wales

When the policymakers and charities noticed this drop, they investigated in the hope of identifying the cause. There were lots of ideas but few answers. Public health officials hypothesised that it could have been everything from increased living standards to a higher uptake of the Samaritans Helpline. However, little evidence showed whether any of their hypotheses had resulted in the reduction.

The most common way to commit suicide in the early 20th century was to place your head in a domestic oven and switch on the gas. Coal gas contains lots of carbon monoxide, which combines irreversibly with the haemoglobin in the blood. With the haemoglobin taken out of action, the blood can't transport oxygen around the body, resulting in asphyxiation and death. Gas poisoning was a simple, clean, effective, and readily available way to commit suicide. It could be done from the comfort of your own home, and hundreds of people did so every year.

Natural gas, however, doesn't have the same effect. It contains lots of methane but hardly any carbon monoxide, so whilst it may give you the mother of all headaches, it won't kill you. Public health officials concluded that, by removing the means to commit suicide, the gas transformation had stopped hundreds of deaths.

The idea that replacing coal gas caused a reduction in suicides was refuted strongly. As the critics pointed out, there are thousands of ways to kill yourself. Anybody motivated to commit suicide could jump off a bridge just as easily as put their head in an oven. But they were wrong. It isn't nearly as easy to jump off a bridge as stick your head in your oven. You must find a bridge and persuade yourself to jump off it. All the other methods of suicide: hanging, shooting or drowning, are significantly more complicated (and frightening) than putting your head in an oven.

When the statisticians stripped out the number of deaths due to carbon monoxide poisoning, it became clear that the switch to natural gas saved lives. The change in gas supply had inadvertently made it much harder for people to do the wrong thing.

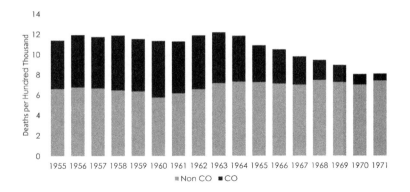

Figure 15: Suicide Rates Involving Carbon Monoxide (CO)

Both stories demonstrate the most powerful way to change people's behaviour and ensure your improvement or learning sticks is to create an environment or system where it is easy to do the right thing and hard to get things wrong. It is all a question of good design. A prominent example is the three-pin plug which only goes into a socket one way. You must try quite hard to electrocute yourself.

Another example is the Google home page. Arguably, Google is the most powerful website on the planet, yet all the user has to do is type their search query into the big empty box in the middle of the screen. My daughters have used all that power with aplomb since they were four.

Quality of design does, however, cut both ways. Plenty of products are so poor that you can't help but get things wrong. My pet peeve is my car. I bought a Volvo.* They are reputedly the safest cars in the world, yet a poorly designed (but very sexy-looking) touchscreen display controls the heating, cooling, navigation and entertainment. When I was cold in my first car (which I bought in 1989), I reached out my hand and turned a

*It is the middle-aged, middle-class thing to do and gives a smug sense of social superiority. I recommend it.

knob to one of three settings. Now I stare at a screen and fiddle with the control while trying to determine if I would be more comfortable at 20 or 20.5 degrees Celsius, when what I really should be doing is looking at the road in front of me. Haptics (the perception of objects by touch) is a much-overlooked way of making things easy to get right. Remember the story of Alphonse Chapanis and the Boeing B-17 Flying Fortress.

In Volvo's defence, they did invent the three-point safety belt and let every other manufacturer use this simple yet revolutionary safety device (another example of great design that makes it easy for people to do the right thing.) Volvo is simply keeping pace with the market. They would struggle to sell a car with a simple tactile heating knob when their competitors sell all-singing, all-dancing computer screens.

Humans love technology, and we can be our own worst enemies. The management challenge is to design solutions humans find simple (and desirable) to use.

Battling Human Nature

Road safety is a fascinating example of an issue where many have tried to build in lessons from accidents, change behaviour and stop things from going wrong. Engineers and civil servants have developed and instigated numerous error-proof systems. These include (to name but two), anti-lock braking systems to reduce the frequency of collisions, and cycling helmets to reduce the severity of cycling injuries.

Neither of these interventions worked as well as expected. During the 1980s, two German scientists studied the effectiveness of antilock-braking systems (ABS) by following a fleet of taxicabs in Munich. As this was the 1980s, ABS wasn't widespread. Some taxis were fitted with the innovation, and others had conventional braking systems. The researchers discovered that the crash rates for the cars with ABS were marginally worse (though not statistically so) than those without. The error-proofed vehicles were no safer to ride in.[112]

In 1998, another research team studied cycling injuries, working their way through the accident statistics of US cyclists. They found that bicycle-related fatalities are positively and significantly associated with increased helmet use.[113] If Americans wore helmets, they were more likely to die on the roads. In this case, not only did the fail-safe innovation fail, but it also made things far worse.

The scientists devised the "risk compensation" theory to explain what was happening. It suggests that people adjust their behaviour depending on the amount of risk they perceive. The riskier a situation appears, the more carefully they behave. The opposite, however, is also true. The German taxi drivers felt safer knowing they wouldn't skid, so they took more risks. A far worse outcome was that American car drivers overtaking cyclists wearing helmets thought them less vulnerable, so they gave them less space.

There is some debate about the validity of the risk compensation theory. Still, it does highlight another option if you want to implement systems that reinforce learning and reduce the likelihood of errors. The first is to build safer systems – make it easy for your staff to get it right. The second is to increase the perceived risk – make your staff more cautious.

Public health provides an example of both approaches being brought to bear on a problem. In the UK, the proportion of adults that smoke has dropped significantly since the 1970s.[114]

This reduction is an impressive example of public health policy in action. Assuming smoking counts as a mistake (and as one of those who has quit, I can tell you it is), this is a very successful case of learning, behavioural change and error reduction. There have been a host of interventions that civil servants and politicians have instigated, and they fall into both camps:

Build safer systems:

- Sell e-cigarettes.
- Ban smoking in public places.
- Raise taxes.
- Prohibit tobacco advertising.
- Ban cigarette vending machines.
- Provide nicotine patches.

Increase the perceived risk:

- Put graphic images of smoking-related diseases on packages.
- Replace branding with blunt messages "Smoking can cause a slow and painful death."
- Invest in no-holds-barred television awareness campaigns.

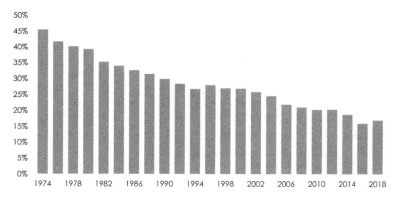

Figure 16: Proportion of UK Adults That Smoke

Over 40 years, using a combination of methods, the UK public health authorities have halved the number of smokers in the country, reducing them by approximately 15 million. To repeat

Ackoff's terminology, to dissolve the problem, you must tackle it in many ways.

Progress and productivity come from learning and applying that knowledge through increasingly more sophisticated and subtle interventions. Facilitating that progress is the role of a manager, yet the focus of most managers' daily lives has little to do with learning and improving systems and everything to do with managing perception and hitting targets.

Summary
Key Points

- There are four ways to solve a problem: absolve, resolve, solve or dissolve. They become progressively more successful.
- Human beings are fallible, always have been, and always will be. Training, incentives and discipline are poor ways to maintain organisational learning.
- Don't overlook low-tech approaches. Checklists, if they are well-designed and their use is reinforced, can be miraculous.
- Build in learning by designing error-proof and fail-safe systems. The better the system design, the less likely failures will occur.
- Humans compensate for risk. If we believe something is safe, we become complacent. Ensure that people understand the danger of what they are doing.
- Proactive managers constantly build controls to lock in progress. If you don't develop better controls, you won't improve. Dissolving problems is the most productive thing a manager can do.

Actions

- If your organisation has a list of historic "things gone wrong", run through the list and see what mechanisms and controls have been put in place to stop problems from reoccurring.
- If the fix was training, design a better fix that doesn't rely on people.
- If the fix was systematic, test it to see if it still works. If it doesn't, fix the fix.
- If you don't have a list of things gone wrong and operational controls, write one.

Chapter 9:
A Columbo Moment

Better Never Rests

During the 1970s, there was a television series starring Frank Columbo, a shrewd Los Angeles homicide detective.* He wore a rumpled beige raincoat, had an unassuming manner, drove an old car, and his apparent ineptitude meant that murderers consistently underestimated him. He would invariably say, "just one more thing…" before asking a critical question and solving the case.

The just one more thing to remember is that the learning cycles are iterative. Putting in place a mechanism that locks in enhanced productivity is good, but as the adage goes, "better never rests". Sustained progress only comes from continuous improvement and not one-off actions.

> *When you think you have tried everything, you haven't.*
>
> *~ Thomas Edison*

---

* Columbo's first name has never been officially confirmed, but Frank has appeared on his ID throughout the series. (Hat tip to Jakki Bendell)

Part 4.

Curating Culture

Chapter 10:
Management Behaving Badly

Problems With Schools and Hospitals

So far, this book has been common sense. The observation that, for an organisation to thrive, it must learn and develop, is not a radical insight. Yet just because something is common sense doesn't mean it is common practice. Learning and improving are not the default modes in many businesses.

A Toxic Culture

In large organisations, behaviour and culture reflect the desires and wants of the senior executives. Those managers may well be more focused on their own personal financial gain than the corporation's success. Whilst learning might be good for an organisation, it isn't necessarily the easiest route for those at the top.

In 2011, a state report to the governor's office in Georgia claimed there was "organised and systemic misconduct" in 44 of Atlanta's 56 public schools.[115] Two years later, 35 teachers, head teachers and administrative staff were brought to trial and charged with racketeering (dishonest and fraudulent business dealings) and other offences.[116]

The accusations revolved around "wrong-to-right erasures" in the Criterion-Referenced Competency Tests (CRCT).* A wrong-to-right erasure is a correction in a multiple-choice test from a wrong

---

*These are annual academic ability exams in elementary and middle schools which tests students' maths, English, art, social studies and science abilities.

answer to a right one. These corrections are always found on test papers as students go back over their answers at the end of the exam and check them, but the number of modifications that inspectors found in Atlanta was extreme. The state prosecutor, Fani Willis, told the jury that a person was more likely to be hit by lightning twice in the same week than there be this volume of changes.

> "What you are going to learn is that in 2009 there were 256,769,000 wrong-to-right erasures… Do you know what the odds of such wrong-to-right erasures are? One in a quadrillion. That's 15 zeros. A quadrillion."[117] *

In 2009 the Atlanta Journal-Constitution published a story about striking rises in test scores at West Manor and Peyton Forest elementary schools.[118] The journalists challenged whether the rising scores could be so dramatic. When presented with the allegations, Georgia Governor Sonny Perdue investigated what had happened. It was no small task as cheating in the school system had become widespread. By the time the enquiry was complete, over 60 investigators had interviewed more than 2,100 people and looked at more than 800,000 documents. They reported a litany of facts and figures:

- 178 teachers were involved in cheating.
- 38 of these were head teachers.
- 82 teachers confessed to the allegations.
- One principal forced a teacher with low CRCT scores to crawl under a table at a faculty meeting.

---

*I'm a bit startled by this number. The population of Atlanta is roughly half a million people. Assuming one in 10 are of school age (50,000), 256 million erasures equate to over 5,000 per child (and they won't all have been sitting the test). Perhaps I shouldn't believe everything I read in the papers.

- Teachers arranged seating for tests so lower-performing children could copy the higher-scoring students' answers.
- Teachers pointed to the correct answer while standing at students' desks.

The New Yorker picked up the story and fleshed it out with some details behind the headlines.[119] A teacher would steal a single paper when the tests were delivered to schools. They would take the test and prepare an answer key on a transparency sheet. Once the exams were over, the teachers would use the key to make corrections. One group explained that they took the papers to a teacher's home and had a "changing party". Another teacher admitted that she had changed test results in 2006, 2007, 2008 and 2009. Yet another teacher described how students who fell asleep or refused to complete the exam still met or exceeded the test's expectations.

The story is shocking but doesn't sound so bad (what harm did it do?) until you realise the authorities denied many children special educational assistance because their falsely reported CRCT scores were too high.

The CRCT test scores were essential to Georgia's compliance with the "No Child Left Behind Act", passed by the US administration in 2002. The legislation was an attempt to raise education levels across the States. The government expected schools to achieve "adequate yearly progress", and the target ratcheted up annually. Those schools that didn't improve their test scores were subject to remedial actions. These ranged from school improvement plans to staff replacement and potential closure.[120]

Three years before the act, Atlanta had appointed a new head of education (the Atlanta Public Schools Superintendent), Beverley L. Hall. Ms Hall was well respected for her work turning around schools in New York and New Jersey. She promoted a "data-

driven" system. Her mantra was "no exceptions, no excuses".
Hall's approach appeared to work. To the outside world, Atlanta's
public schools went from strength to strength, so much so that in
2009, the American Association of School Administrators named
Ms Hall the "National Superintendent of the Year".

Inside the Atlanta school system, the reality was different. Ms
Hall ran a closed hierarchical organisation. Most of her employees
needed special permission to enter her central offices. Those that
did and bumped into her kept their mouths shut and greeted her
with just a smile or a nod.

Hall linked teacher evaluations to test scores to ensure she met
government targets. She warned principals that she would fire
them if they didn't meet their targets. Eventually, Hall replaced
90% of her head teachers. One principal claimed, "The way
principals keep their jobs in Atlanta is they make targets." Whistle-
blowers who reported the cheating to Hall's aides were ridiculed
and punished, while school staff who beat the exam targets were
given cash bonuses (even the bus drivers and dinner ladies). At the
same time, Hall's pay grew to a base salary of nearly $300,000 per
year and a bonus that, over 10 years, netted her a further half a
million dollars. These bonuses were also primarily linked to test
score results.

The governor's investigators concluded, "Hall created an
atmosphere that rewarded cheaters, punished whistle-blowers and
covered up wrongdoing."[121] Whilst they stopped short of claiming
that Ms Hall had directed anybody to cheat, they did claim that Ms
Hall "created a culture of fear, intimidation and retaliation" that
had allowed "cheating — at all levels — to go unchecked for
years."

The legal proceedings that followed the investigation took six
months, and ultimately the court convicted 11 teachers of
racketeering. Twenty-one others pleaded guilty to receive shorter

sentences. The judge didn't pass sentence on Beverley Hall as she was too ill to face trial and died of cancer before proceedings ended.

It is easy to explain this as a single event caused by a bad apple. However, there have been reports of cheating to hit the No Child Left Behind targets across the United States, in cities including St Louis, Houston, Cincinnati, Baltimore, El Paso and Philadelphia.[122] In the UK, where the government has used targets widely to drive educational performance, there have also been accusations of teachers bribing pupils before school inspections.[123]

Following the Atlanta case and criticism of the act, the US Government has replaced "No Child Left Behind" with "Every Student Succeeds". This legislation still maintains the "hallmark annual standardized testing requirements". Only time will tell if the new act prevents further dysfunctional behaviour. Yet, if it is in the interests of senior managers to cheat the system, it would be naive to assume it won't happen again.

A Complacent Culture

Organisations don't have to be as dishonest or brutal as the Atlanta Public Schools system for things to go awry. Simple inattention and loss of focus can be equally disastrous.

In February 2001, 18-year-old Wayne Jowett died while receiving leukaemia treatment at the Queen's Medical Centre in Nottingham. The chemotherapy consisted of two medicines: Cytosine, a drug injected directly into the spinal fluid and Vincristine, a drug that medics inject into the patient's blood. The doctor on duty that day, Dr Feda Mulhem, made a mistake. Instead of injecting the Vincristine into Wayne's vein, he asked a junior doctor to inject it into his spine.

It was a fatal error. Vincristine is a potent chemical – it can be deadly when injected into the spinal column. The hospital staff soon noticed their mistake and desperately attempted to reverse the treatment, but to no avail. Slowly, Wayne became paralysed. It was a hopeless situation. One month after the accident, medical staff turned off his life support systems, and Wayne Jowett died. As Wayne was under the supervision of Dr Mulhem, the doctor was tried for manslaughter and ultimately received an eight-month sentence after admitting his failure.

Wayne's father was justifiably distraught: "Eight months for the killing of my son is absolutely ridiculous. It leaves a sour taste in my mouth."[124] The health service had let down the Jowett family shamefully.

The tragedy occurred after a series of failures in a complicated procedure:

- Wayne Jowett was understandably nervous about the treatment and was late for his appointment at the hospital.
- Nobody contacted his regular physician (who had left for the day) when Wayne arrived despite his asking to be called.
- The two drugs should have been administered to the patient on separate days. They weren't.
- Likewise, the two drugs should have been delivered to the ward on different days. They weren't.
- It was Dr Mulhem's second day on this job.
- Dr Mulhem had never been formally trained in the use of Vincristine.
- Dr Mulhem didn't read the medical chart properly.[125]

A subsequent investigation into the tragedy discovered over 30 different failures in the system.[126] If any of those mishaps hadn't occurred, it could have prevented Wayne Jowett's death. But all the errors coincided.

Accident prevention experts call it the "Swiss Cheese Effect". Imagine a packet of slices of Swiss cheese (the one with holes) in a supermarket. Usually, you can't see through the tray, but it is possible for all the holes to line up, in which case daylight will flood through. Likewise, if errors line up, accidents occur.

During the 2017 Oscar Awards, a series of errors lined up and caused Brian Cullinan's blushes. Similarly, but far more tragically, all the holes in the medical system lined up simultaneously, and a deadly accident happened. Yes, the doctor was responsible for one of those holes. He made a mistake. He wasn't the only one, we all make mistakes.

Compounding the tragedy was the fact that this was not the first time (or last) that medical staff administered Vincristine incorrectly. The same mistake had been made in UK hospitals on 13 occasions over the previous 15 years, with fatal consequences. Preventing the accident was relatively easy. After the incident, the chief medical officer commissioned Professor Brian Toft, a specialist in patient safety and root cause analysis, to investigate Wayne Jowett's death. He recommended developing a new spinal needle that could not fit intravenous syringes. This change would error-proof the procedure. However, as he later told a parliamentary health committee:

> "The most critical recommendation made in my report following Wayne Jowett's death is still outstanding seven years later."[127]

In 2004, three years after the Nottingham tragedy, Guido Squillaci died in the same way in Australia.[128] Deaths have also occurred in the US (2005), Spain (2005) and Hong Kong (2007). The WHO repeated the same recommendation as Professor Toft to prevent inadvertent injections by:

"Making it physically impossible to attach an intravenous syringe containing vincristine to a spinal needle ('lock and key design')."

In 2014, 13 years after Professor Toft's recommendation, NHS England issued a stage three patient safety alert (a directive) that asked hospitals to confirm that they had implemented the error-proof design and warned of regulatory action if they had not. [129]

It is human nature to seek somebody out to blame, hold accountable and punish when things go wrong. Hence, it is in senior managers' interests to be fed a scapegoat so they can be seen to be taking firm action (also deflecting the blame from themselves). But a culture where that is normal behaviour won't improve.

Everybody makes mistakes and punishing them after the event won't stop the errors from reoccurring. It is as pointless as closing the stable door after the horse has bolted. The situation is exacerbated, though, as blame and punishment make errors more likely.

In organisations where it is the norm to blame people, staff are scared of the consequences of a mistake. As they fear recrimination, they will not admit it when they make a an error. Instead, they cover issues up. As problems are swept under the carpet, no record exists. Consequently, nobody realises how big those problems are or how often they arise and organisations don't take steps to address them.

Four doctors had already been prosecuted for manslaughter for the same error when Dr Mulhem made his fatal mistake.[130] Not one of those prosecutions saved Wayne Jowett. Until the system changed, patients continued to die.

> *A bad system will beat a good person every time.*
>
> ~ W. Edwards Deming

Postscript

I originally wrote about Wayne Jowett and Feda Mulhem in a blog post. A year after I published it, somebody left this comment:

> "Dr Mulhem is my uncle.
> And a few years after this incident
> His whole world collapsed
> And he committed suicide
> I miss him."

Managers and politicians could have averted a double tragedy if they had created a culture that embraced, learnt from, and acted upon mistakes. It took 13 years to implement Professor Toft's recommendation. The press hasn't reported Dr Mulhem's suicide.

Summary

Key Points

- Culture has been defined as "the way we do things around here."
- Unsurprisingly the way we do things affects outcomes.
- Culture comes from the top of the organisation and percolates down.
- In a poor culture:
    - There is a definite hierarchy.
    - Managers are unapproachable.
    - Managers are more worried about their position than organisational performance.
    - Managers use bullying, threats and fear to control their staff.

- ○ Managers drive performance by issuing targets.
- ○ Managers don't care how staff meet their targets.
- ○ Whistle-blowers are punished.
- ○ Scapegoats are routinely found and slaughtered.
- ○ Learning isn't sought or acted upon.
- In these cultures, problems are hidden or ignored, and cheating occurs.

Actions

- W. Edwards Deming said that managers should **"Drive out fear"**. The challenge is to drive fear out of your organisation and replace it with an open, collaborative culture.
- Run a culture audit. Ask your staff to tell you what it is like to work in your organisation. There are plenty of internet resources that will help.
- As a manager, stop asking, **"Who** caused that?" and move to **"What** caused that?"
- Start with your part of the organisation. You cannot influence everything.
- Find another organisation if yours won't support you. Life is too short to work in a dysfunctional culture.

Chapter 11:
A Bad Idea That Refuses to Die

Why HR Shouldn't be Trusted to Manage People

If an organisation deliberately wanted to build a dysfunctional culture, one of the most effective ways would be to create an environment where managers pit employees against each other. This could be done by creating a high-stakes game of reward and failure where senior managers used targets and goals to judge their employees' relative abilities. By doing this, an organisation could ensure that employees were constantly competing for bonuses or scared for their jobs. This process would motivate them to play all the dysfunctional cards: cheating to hit targets, blaming and bullying others, hiding issues and telling managers what they want to hear (a "good news" culture).

Whilst this sounds idiotic, it is precisely what many, if not most, large corporations do. The root cause of many businesses' cultural problems is how they manage their people. It is as if they have intentionally broken their organisation.

Employee Performance Management

Traditional management wisdom is that we should set stretching goals and targets, measure employees' performance against those goals, and managers should provide frequent feedback. Managers supercharge the approach with extrinsic motivators – either a bonus (carrot) or the threat of job loss (stick) to motivate people to do well. This procedure allows an organisation to weed out the poorly performing employees, constantly "raising the bar" and improving the quality and calibre of its workforce. Managers should enforce this process rigorously via an annual cycle of objective setting and calibration, mid-year reviews and end-of-year performance validation and appraisals, all underpinned by continuous feedback and "quality conversations".

At its most extreme (although not uncommon), this logic leads organisations to apply a "vitality curve" or "forced distribution" to its staff, as popularised by Jack Welch at General Electric (GE) in the 1980s. A defined proportion of the organisation, its lowest performers, are told their services are no longer required every year, so improving the average performance of the organisation as a whole. Whilst this "performance management" is a seductive idea, the logic has several flaws.

Flaw #1: Ranking Performance is (Almost) Impossible

The NHS developed an approach to enhance clinical performance and patient care. The strapline for the programme is *"Data for Better Services"*. The organisation started to publish metrics that show individual consultants' mortality rates. Before a patient sees a specialist, they can visit an online portal to see if the doctor has a high death rate associated with the medical care they provide. The premise behind this transparency is that it allows the public to hold their medical practitioners accountable. If they don't like the information they see, they can vote with their feet and find another doctor.[131]

At face value, this is an excellent idea. It is straightforward to measure consultants' performance by counting the number of deaths they are associated with (notwithstanding the earlier points about Covid-19 mortality rates), so the data should be precise and the related performance ranking unambiguous.

The data is split by the consultant's speciality. I downloaded one set of data to create this chart. It shows the mortality rate by number of cardiac surgeons.

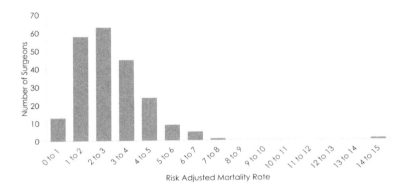

Figure 17: Mortality Rate Ranking of Cardiac Surgeons

Statisticians have given each surgeon a "risk-adjusted mortality rate". As you can see, some surgeons kill more patients than others (a cheap but apparently not unfounded shot).

I'm a man in his mid-fifties and may need cardiac surgery, so personally, the inference is obvious: I should only visit a surgeon who scores 0 to 1 point. I'd be willing to travel to the far tip of Scotland if that is where those surgeons practise. With luck, it won't be every day that I will have a heart bypass. Why would I, or anybody else, want the procedure carried out by an "average" surgeon? My other conclusion from the data is that the last person I want to see is the surgeon with 14 points on the far right. If I interpret the information correctly, it should be invaluable when choosing a surgeon.

In reality, the individual performance data is meaningless. The first issue is that half of the data was missing; only 214 of the 398 surgeons listed were given a score. It isn't clear from the information whether this is because the surgeons didn't have any deaths to their name, hadn't practised enough surgical operations, the data was corrupt, or the statisticians lost count.

The second issue is that according to the NHS statisticians, every surgeon (even the one with 14 points) was "within the expected range", that is, there was no indication of statistical significance. The data shows a variation in mortality rate, which is not the same as saying that some surgeons kill more people than others. If I asked all these surgeons to flip a coin 100 times, some would flip substantially more heads than others. That doesn't make them better coin flippers; it just means that chance variation altered outcomes. The same is true for mortality rates. It is hard to tell what is real and what is random noise. When the statisticians say they were "within the expected range", they mean that the difference in scores is just down to luck. I read that as the surgeons are all the same.

Finally, although the data is risk-adjusted (though what that means is not defined), there was no indication of context. If we assume that the scores of the surgeons were different (despite the analyst's assertion that they are statistically the same), the data doesn't tell me why they were different. The doctor with 14 points may be the best surgeon in the country, so he undertakes the trickiest operations. He might also work with a cack-handed anaesthetist who turns up to work drunk, or his catchment area could be the fast food, cigarette and booze-fuelled cardiac arrest capital of the UK. Each of these would explain why his performance is so poor and has nothing to do with the surgeon. Without context, there is no way of knowing. The publishers of the data admit that:

"When mortality rates are higher than expected, there are several possible explanations which include issues with the data, abnormal case mix which is not adjusted for by the risk models, issues with the hospital's care or issues with the individual surgeon's care. Any judgement can only be made after a full investigation of all the issues."

As a member of the public, I have no chance of making a "full investigation of all the issues". The data is useless to me.

There is also a strong argument that publishing performance data this way detracts from performance. If doctors are penalised (and we have seen that they can be), they will reduce their exposure by only taking on mild cases with little chance of failure, or hiding issues, which means that they don't get resolved. Publishing this data set and ranking the surgeons has far more to do with politicians wanting to look like they are improving performance than with actually improving performance.

> *No physician is excellent until he has killed one or two patients.*
>
> *~ Hindu Proverb*

If it isn't possible to determine individual performance within a single profession, how should you compare the performance between roles in a broader organisation? The solution proposed by HR departments is to measure performance against annual goals. Yet setting arbitrary targets doesn't show how well somebody performed (just how good they are at negotiating a target), and calibrating targets to ensure they are fair and equal is a facile exercise. Comparing an advertising executive's goals against those of an operations manager isn't so much comparing apples and pears as comparing apples and supermarket trolleys.

If measuring performance is futile in the NHS, why would attempting to rank performance be valuable at a bank, bakery, brothel or anywhere else? Performance measurement has more to do with the person holding the tape than the person they are measuring. We all rate people highly if they see the world the same way as us and agree with our ideas and approaches. However, just because you agree with my point of view that doesn't make you (or me) an excellent performer.

When managers claim they can see a difference in performance, they are kidding themselves. All they can see are people they like, who share their perspectives and don't ask awkward or challenging questions. This conformity does nothing for diversity of thought, innovation or productivity.

There are a couple of exceptions to the rule that focusing on individual performance is futile. An example of the first is the case of Dr Harold Shipman (a general practitioner in the UK who is believed to have murdered 250 people). It shows that understanding who the poor performers are and acting on it are very important. However, poor performance of this nature is so far off the scale that it is blindingly obvious when you look for it. It is not "within the expected range". To deal with such wilfully poor performance, seek out the individuals responsible and act. It should be a daily routine to look for malpractice or dishonesty and address it, not a once-every-six-months process of forcing people into ranked boxes.

The second exception is dependent on how managers use the data. The data on the surgeons' performance would be invaluable if it forced the right questions. The health service is measuring variation in the system, not between individual doctors. So, as John Snow asked about the cholera outbreak in 19th century London, and Alphonse Chapanis did about bomber crashes during the Second World War, the question should be "**what** is causing the variation?" not "**who** is causing the problem?"

Perhaps one surgeon has a poor mortality rate because he works from a cottage hospital in deepest rural Wales, and doesn't have access to the drugs and equipment he would find in a large metropolitan teaching hospital. In that case, the way to reduce deaths is to give him the equipment (or send the patients to Cardiff).

Unfortunately, most managers conclude that the surgeon is at fault without understanding the cause. So, they shame him, warn him he might lose his job, and generally put the fear of God into him, which will do anything but enhance performance.

Flaw #2: The Self-Fulfilling Prophecy
Douglas McGregor famously put forward two contrasting world views in his book, *The Human Side of Enterprise*.[132] Summarising them rather bluntly, they are:

- **Theory X**: Workers are lazy, have no interest in working and are only in it for the pay cheque.
- **Theory Y**: Workers are highly motivated and will push themselves to do rewarding work.

Those two worldviews are mutually exclusive and can't both be right. If we had time to collect the data, we would find that workers would tend to behave one way or the other. There should be an average level of engagement that managers could react to. But that wasn't Dr McGregor's point. He wasn't talking about workers' behaviour but about managers' perspectives.

If a manager believes their team is lazy and good for nothing (Theory X), he will check their every move and rebuke them whenever they step out of line. McGregor believed that managers who behave like that discover that the minute they turn their backs, their employees gossip, bitch, moan and do as little work as possible. Conversely, Theory Y managers believe their employees will do the best they can. They give them opportunities, back them to the hilt and praise them for their efforts. Consequently, McGregor hypothesised that when these managers aren't watching, their employees move mountains to finish the work.

The self-fulfilling nature of Theory X and Theory Y was only a hypothesis. Yet subsequent research into a phenomenon known as the "Pygmalion Effect" reinforces the idea.*

> "If a manager is convinced that the people in her group are first-rate, they'll reliably outperform a group whose manager believes the reverse, even if the innate talent of the two groups is similar."[133]

Several experiments have proven the effect. The first was undertaken in the 1960s when two scientists, Rosenthal and Fode, tried to rear intelligent rats.[134] To see if they had been successful, they ran a series of experiments with two strains of rats and a series of mazes. The first strain was "maze bright". The rats' parents and grandparents were good at navigating mazes. The second group was "maze dull". Their ancestors were the couch potatoes of the rat world.

A group of students put the rats through their paces. The rodents had to navigate successive obstacles to find a food cache. The students timed the runs and compiled the results. The experiment was a resounding success. The maze bright rats were faster at negotiating the mazes. There was no statistical doubt. Rosenthal and Fode had bred a clever rat.

There was a fascinating twist to the experiment. Not only were these maze bright rats better at running through mazes, but their handlers also found them more pleasant and likeable. They were far calmer to handle than the maze dull rats and more fun to pet

---

* The name comes from George Bernard Shaw's play *Pygmalion*, where the cockney flower girl, Eliza Doolittle, is trained to act like a duchess.

and play with. This fact suggested a genetic linkage in rats between intellect and demeanour.

The truth is that it was all a big con. There wasn't a breeding programme. The rats were all standard lab rats randomly allocated to the maze bright and maze dull groups. The only difference between them was what the experimenters told the student handlers. This phenomenon is the "Experimenter Effect", an example of a self-fulfilling prophecy. It proves that if the experimenter thinks highly of a rat, it will respond well, whereas if the experimenter has a low opinion of the rat, it will behave poorly. The experiment proved that both "Theory X and Theory Y" apply when handling rats.

Rosenthal continued his studies, pushing the experiment further and applying what he had learned about rats to children.[135] Working with Lenore Jacobson, he was keen to understand why some children overachieved at school and others didn't. The theory they tested was that classroom performance depended on intelligence. The experimenters hypothesised that a child's IQ was a good predictor of how quickly a child would progress, so they ran intelligence tests on children in different classes. With this data, they identified the children who showed "unusual potential for intellectual growth". They sense-checked the results with the teachers to ensure they hadn't missed anything.

Eight months later, Rosenthal and Jacobson returned to the school and asked the children to retake the intelligence tests. Their predictions were correct. The children highlighted as having superior potential showed a marked increase in test scores. The "normal" children didn't fare as well.

Once again, it was a trick. Rosenthal and Jacobson had played the same game as before and randomly allocated children to the potential and normal groups. The increase in performance had nothing to do with the children's intellectual prowess. Instead, it depended on the teacher's belief about a child's potential. If a teacher had been told a child was exceptional, the child became exceptional, another example of the Pygmalion Effect at work. Rosenthal and Jacobson had the ethical sense not to allocate children to a low-potential group. I'll leave it to your imagination what the implications would have been.

Two other psychologists (Eden and Shani) picked up where Rosenthal and Jacobson left off.[136] They wanted to see if the Pygmalion Effect also existed in the military and persuaded the Israeli Government to let them find out. Three times a year, the Israeli Army ran a combat command course. Roughly 100 trainee soldiers were allocated to one of four instructors every term. They subsequently received 16 hours of daily instructor/trainee contact for 15 weeks.

On one occasion, before a group of trainees started the course, Eden and Shani gave them a series of psychometric tests. They also looked at the ratings from each trainee's previous commanders. With this information, they predicted the trainee's "command potential".

- **High Potential**: Scores suggested they would do well as combat commanders.
- **Regular Potential**: Scores met the course requirements but did not exceed them.
- **Unknown Potential**: Scores were not statistically grounded (Eden and Shani wanted to build their credibility by "admitting" that they couldn't predict everything).

The experimenters shared each trainee's potential with their instructors before the course began. The instructors didn't know that Eden and Shani had (like all the experimenters before) randomly allocated the trainee's rating. The rating had nothing to do with their ability. The experimenters only undertook the exercise to manipulate the instructors' expectations.

At the end of the course, the army evaluated the soldiers. They used a set of objective tests that measured speed, accuracy, and learning. The design of the tests removed any biases that the instructors may have developed. Eden and Shani added an extra layer of sophistication to their research. They also asked the trainees to rate their instructors. The score reflected the instructors' leadership ability and the likelihood that trainees would recommend the course.

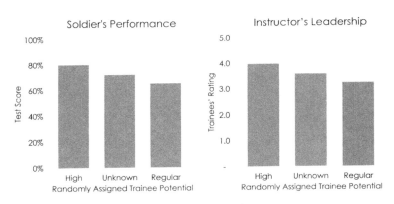

Figure 18: Pygmalion Effect on Soldiers

The first evaluation reinforced the existence of the Pygmalion Effect. The trainees that instructors thought had the most potential did best. If an instructor believed someone would do well, they did.

The soldier's feedback showed that the soldiers allocated to the high potential group rated their instructors most highly. Yet the low potential soldiers ranked the same instructors poorly. These were precisely the same teachers on the same course. The instructor's leadership style varied from soldier to soldier. Eden and Shani theorised that the instructor's demeanour depended on their expectations. They changed their behaviour in line with their perception of the soldier they were working with.

How does the Pygmalion Effect work? Why would a rat, child or soldier do well just because a student, teacher or instructor expected them to? Robert Rosenthal carried out further studies in the classroom that explained how expectations create outcomes.[137] It comes down to four behaviours that most of us display without thinking:

- **Climate:** If a teacher thinks a child is clever, she will act warmly toward the child. She will give the child more eye contact, laugh at the child's jokes and show the child more encouragement. She will make the child feel happy in the classroom.

- **Feedback:** As the (cringe-worthy) phrase goes, "feedback is the breakfast of champions". If a child is to learn, he must know when he got things right and wrong. If a teacher thinks a child is clever, she will give the child both more and varied feedback.

- **Inputs:** Teachers give the children that they expect to succeed more material and different assignments. The challenges are more complex, and the children get extra homework. This additional work may show the child that he is well thought of, or it might give the child no option but to learn more.

- **Outputs:** An output is a chance to show what you have learnt. Answering a question is an output, finishing a project is an output, and reading out loud in class is an output. Teachers give the children they think will do well the opportunity to answer questions and deliver more outputs.

When it is positive, the Pygmalion Effect creates a virtuous spiral. It is easy to understand how some children thrive in school.

They get better and better and achieve more and more. But the spiral works both ways. It is just as easy to imagine a dark side to the Pygmalion Effect and see how other children plod through school. They never achieve anything and drop out. Although few teachers would consciously condemn a child to failure, it is obvious how that could happen.

There are plenty of similarities between teachers, army instructors and managers. They are all trying to improve performance by controlling the working environment. They all provide feedback and hand out assignments. Finally, for good or ill, all three have their favourites.

The vicious and virtuous spirals work the same way in the workplace as anywhere else, so the implication is clear. The way to increase the results from our teams is simple: increase our expectations of those who work for us. We should believe that all our employees will be successful. That will give them (and us) the best chance of turning perception into reality.

However, "ranking and stacking" employees and then publicly labelling half of them as just "meeting" or "below" expectations forces managers to create a group of poor performers. Is it any wonder that they fail? Using performance management to identify poor performers is a self-fulfilling prophecy. Though it doesn't "manage performance", it destroys it.

> *Whether you believe you can do a thing or not, you are right.*
>
> *~ Henry Ford*

Flaw #3: Incentives Work, but Not as You'd Expect

One of the core tenets of the performance management process is the use of incentives. It is common knowledge that if you provide an incentive (invariably a big fat cash bonus), the potential reward will motivate staff to do better. We are convinced that our employees are "coin-operated". The more money we wave in front of them, the harder they will run.

Daniel Pink explores this theme in his book, *Drive*,[138] where he investigates human motivation. Pink shows that incentives work perfectly for repetitive unthinking tasks (think piece work), yet they fall apart for anything more complicated.

One of the experiments he discusses is the "Candle Problem", which was first put forward by the behavioural psychologist Karl Duncker in the 1930s. Duncker asked his subjects to fasten a candle to a wall and light it. He provided them with a candle, a box of matches and some thumbtacks, then timed the action to see how long it took them to solve the problem. Those involved would attempt several things, tacking the candle to the wall or using candle wax as an adhesive before they happened across the solution, which was to use the match box. Once they had realised that the box was part of the solution and not just there to hold the matches, it was a piece of cake to use it as a tray, tack it to the wall and stand the candle up in it. All the answer required was a mental leap from box as packaging to box as solution. It was a real-life case of having to think outside the box (sorry, I couldn't help myself).

In the early 1960s, another psychologist, Sam Glucksberg, used the puzzle as the basis of an investigation into incentives.[139] He recruited two groups of people and timed how long it took them to complete the puzzle. The first group provided a baseline, while the second group was incentivised to enhance performance. Members of that group were told that if they were in the top 25%, they would get a $5 reward, and the fastest would win $25. As this was over 50 years ago, it was a substantial bonus for completing a small task.

Glucksberg's results were fascinating. The baseline group took roughly seven and a half minutes to realise that the box was part of the solution. Yet the incentivised group took over 11 minutes. Counterintuitively, the performance-enhancing incentive slowed the activity by three and a half minutes or some 50%. The explanation for this result is that an incentive causes us to concentrate on the problem, yet to solve many creative problems, we need to be able to shift our focus away from the issue and see other possibilities. In 21st century Europe and America, relatively few of us have entirely routine jobs. Even call centre jobs, regarded as the most menial work, require considerable problem-solving and lateral thinking to resolve customers' problems. If your team codes software solutions, searches for tax loopholes, or is trying to develop the perfect marketing campaign, their work is predominately creative. Precisely the type of work that incentives slow and inhibit.

A second group of psychologists ran experiments to understand the effect of incentives on nursery school children.[140] The children were given different toys and tasks throughout the day, from building blocks and cooking utensils to outdoor games and equipment, to keep them entertained. Some activities were always there whilst others were swapped around, ensuring that the children always had something new to do.

The scientists wanted to understand the impact of incentives on children's motivation, so they provided them with paper and fancy magic markers (this was the 1970s and magic markers were quite exciting). The scientists then sat behind a one-way mirror and recorded how much time the children spent drawing and colouring rather than playing with the other toys and activities.

Once they had created a baseline level of engagement, nursery teachers invited the children to draw pictures. The children were split into three randomly allocated groups. The first group were asked to draw a picture. The second group were told that if they participated, they would get a "good player award"; this was a card with a big gold star, a bright red ribbon and their name written upon it. If you have children, you will have seen something similar. The child could then pin the award to a noticeboard. The final group weren't offered the gold star but received it after they had completed the drawing.

A couple of weeks after the experiment, the team returned with their stopwatches and one-way mirror, laid out the magic markers, and recorded how much time the children spent playing with the drawing equipment again. They discovered that the children who had been told they would receive a big gold star had lost interest in drawing. In contrast, those who didn't receive one, or received it after the event, continued to play with the drawing equipment with the same enthusiasm.

The experimenters had demonstrated the "Overjustification Effect". It occurs when an external incentive, such as a bonus or a big gold star, reduces somebody's intrinsic motivation to perform a task. The message for parents is that whilst it may be sensible to bribe your child to clean their bedroom (I have two teenage daughters, and neither of them has any intrinsic motivation to tidy up), it is unwise to offer them the same reward to read a book or study for their exams. Once the bribe (or bonus or gold star) is taken off the table, motivation slumps. The organisational implication is similar. Once you start offering rewards and incentives to your staff to do things they are already motivated to do, like fixing operational issues, teaching children, or resolving customers' complaints, the incentive becomes the table stake. Once you stop paying the "discretionary bonus", performance will plummet.

In addition to measuring children's engagement, as a side experiment, the psychologists asked a group of judges to rate the quality of the pictures the children completed. They were scored from 1 (very poor) to 5 (very good). The average quality score for the children who knew they were working for a gold star was 2.18 versus an average of 2.77 for the two groups that weren't expecting a reward. The children became more focused on the carrot dangled before them than their pictures.

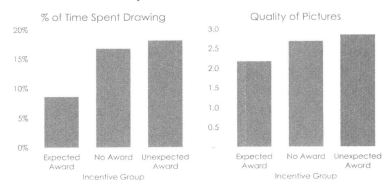

Figure 19: Effect of Incentives on Children

Both experiments demonstrate that conditional external incentives hurt the performance of all but the most simple and repetitive tasks. But what about the employees who didn't receive a reward, particularly when they believed they should?

Frans de Waal is a Dutch zoologist who studies the behaviour of mammals, particularly primates. He gave a fascinating TED talk about his investigations into fairness in the animal world.[141] As part of the talk he showed an experiment involving two capuchin monkeys who worked side by side in a test chamber.

The monkeys were tasked with passing a stone to the researcher, for which they received a reward. At first, the monkeys were given a piece of cucumber every time they handed over a stone. The monkeys thought this a fair deal and were prepared to repeat the trade 25 times. Then the scientist gave one of the monkeys a grape instead of a piece of cucumber (monkeys, like most humans, prefer grapes to cucumber). This was done in full view of the second monkey. When the second monkey was only handed a piece of cucumber for his efforts, he checked that his next stone was what it should have been and then, believing that he was being mistreated, he threw the piece of cucumber back at the scientist in disgust.

For monkeys, not receiving a bonus for your efforts when you believe you should have done, is profoundly demotivating. Frans de Waal showed a video of the experiment in his talk. I defy you to watch the experiment and tell me that what is true for monkeys isn't also the case for humans.*

The third flaw of the performance management process is that incentives have many unforeseen side effects. For all but the most menial tasks, they slow performance, destroy motivation and demoralise those who don't receive them.

A Colossal Waste of Time

There is, however, one overarching issue with performance management that transcends all the flaws in the process. Individual performance is inconsequential for any organisation larger than a handful of people. Consequently, all the effort put into forced rankings is a waste of time and a huge opportunity cost.

High-performing individuals are great, but as any manager will tell you, having a high-performing team is better. Conventional wisdom is that the simplest way to get a high-performing team is to invest in the best-of-breed. Business leaders should find the most capable salespeople, ops guys, marketers and

*Do it now. Search online for "Frans de Waal moral behaviour in animals". There is a three minute video clip. You will love it.

technical wizards and stick them together. Once you have the best individuals, you will have the best team. This logic reinforces the focus on performance management, ranking and stacking, 360-degree feedback, SMART goals and ultimately "pay for performance". To create the most productive team, an organisation must understand who its best performers are and weed out the rest.

A group of researchers led by Alex "Sandy" Pentland from MIT's Human Dynamics Laboratory had a different theory. With a firm nod to Russell L. Ackoff's automobile experiment, they believed that it wasn't the members of the team that made it high performing and gave it the "It Factor", but how they interacted.[142]

To test the theory, they developed electronic badges for people to wear that measured how they worked together. These badges recorded communication in many ways. They could tell whether people faced one another, how much they gestured, talked, listened and interrupted. They also recorded the tone of voice and levels of extroversion and empathy.

The team took their badges and used them to collect information about many different workplaces, from hospital wards to retail banks. They then added data on e-mail traffic, meetings and calls. They studied 21 organisations over seven years, measuring the communication patterns of over 2,500 people. Ultimately, the researchers collated so much data that they claimed to have started a new science, "Sociometrics", or the study of group interactions. The researchers were able to correlate high-performing teams with three aspects of communication:

- **Energy**: The number and nature of exchanges.
- **Engagement**: How evenly team members communicate with one another.
- **Exploration**: The amount of time that the team spend communicating externally.

It turns out that high-performing teams interact differently. This behaviour manifests itself in many ways. They talk to each other rather than firing out e-mails. Face-to-face is even better than the phone. Whilst they communicate powerfully, they don't overdo it, and the boss isn't overbearing; he listens as well as speaks. Strong teams spend time outside their immediate team, bringing and incorporating new ideas into their plans. They also mix socially, as doing so helps break down barriers between people. Conversely, some teams struggle to act coherently. This is particularly true of groups separated by distance, language and culture.

The study went on to describe the best managers as more energetic. They talk more, but they also listen more. They spend more face-to-face time with others. They pick up cues, draw people out and help them to be more outgoing. It's not just what they project that makes them charismatic. It's what they elicit.

The researchers suggested two ways to develop team communication and coordination. The first was high-tech. It is possible to hire the academics who put together the study. They will provide organisations and teams with badges and demonstrate (via some very impressive visualisations) how well a team interacts and what they could do differently.

Alternatively, there are some more straightforward options:

- Change the workspace to have more communal areas and fewer enclosed offices.
- Set up regular face-to-face meetings rather than e-mail cascades.
- Allow teams to go on their break together, giving them time to socialise.
- Gather feedback about management behaviour and tell overbearing bosses to shut up.

Whilst it would be easy to argue that this wasn't an insightful set of observations, the study did point out one less intuitive fact.

"Individual reasoning and talent contribute far less to team success than one might expect. The best way to build a great team is not to select individuals for their smarts or accomplishments but to learn how they communicate and to shape and guide the team so that it follows successful communication patterns."

It doesn't matter how much time you spend finding the best individuals. Creating an environment where they communicate, cooperate and collaborate is much more effective.

Pentland's work with teams and Deming's red bead experiment highlight three different levels at which it is possible to improve the performance of an organisation:

- **Individuals:** The people in the organisation
- **Interactions:** How well the individuals work as a team.
- **Systems:** The processes and infrastructure that hold it together.

Managers focus their performance management efforts on people or individuals. This fact isn't surprising; we are human and conditioned to see and respond to individuals. People's behaviour is the first and most obvious thing we see.

As Pentland showed, a second and more significant driver of performance is how these people interact. Some of this is apparent to us, we can sense team dynamics, yet some is below the waterline and challenging to notice.

The most significant driver is the system that underpins an organisation. At its simplest, a one-person window cleaner would be at a loss if he misplaced his notebook of customers and their needs. When those systems are scaled up to a more significant business, a chain of drive-through restaurants or a multinational bank for example, the power of the systems in determining organisational performance is immense. When something breaks, people run around like scalded cats trying to fix it. If an application decides it has had enough, a data file becomes corrupt, or something as humdrum as a roller door fails in a factory, you will see a stream of people trying to fix it before customers start complaining. Yet if somebody leaves an organisation, it is almost as if they were never there.

People work in teams, and teams build systems, so these three things are interlinked. But managing the people, not the system, is akin to managing the tail and not the dog.

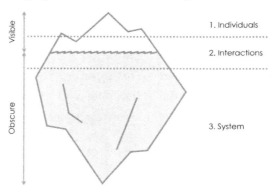

Figure 20: Productivity Iceberg

The Perversity of Performance Management

Even though systems have a more significant effect on performance than people, there are, of course, some individuals who have a more material impact than others. The chief executive officer, the chairman or the chief operating officer can set a direction or a tone that will boost or cripple an organisation. They have far more sway than a software engineer or shift supervisor. Yet perversely, those at the top of the organisation sit in judgement and hand out the grades. It is rare for chief executives to turn the tables and ask the workers to rate their performance.

If you still believe performance management is invaluable, consider your last performance appraisal. Was it a productive experience? Did you tell your manager the cold hard truth and agree with his feedback? Or did you shine the best possible light on your performance and implicate others when things went awry? What would your employees say about their last performance appraisal with you?

The managers in HR who promote these practices know little about how people behave, yet they should be the experts. Institutionalised rating and feedback systems linked to financial rewards or the threat of job losses destroy performance.

How Should you Manage your People?

It is easy to say that the traditional HR methods of performance-rated pay, SMART objectives and performance ranking don't work, but what should you do instead?

The first, rather glib, answer is to stop and not worry about replacing them. They cause more harm than good – you would be better off without them. Most managers could manage their businesses and projects without the "help" provided by their HR departments.

A more conciliatory answer is to break the processes up so they don't create the systematic damage they would otherwise do. Many HR processes are bundled together into the annual review. It is designed to:

- Motivate employees.
- Encourage feedback and communication.
- Provide coaching.

- Set strategy and objectives.
- Allocate performance-related pay.
- Evaluate promotion prospects.
- Make redundancy decisions.
- Discipline staff.
- Provide a paper trail for dealing with poor performers.

By breaking up the activity, an organisation can move away from one overwhelming überprocess to a set of more manageable subtasks. There is no rule that an organisation must pay for performance, have an annual round of promotions, or link organisational strategy to individual performance reviews. It is simply a management fad. Some organisations do things in different ways. Of the six multinationals I have worked for, the most effective didn't pay for individual performance. When I joined, I thought it was nuts, yet this policy killed nearly all the petty jealousies and a host of organisational politics.

There are several high-profile examples of organisations that have ditched their forced ranking process including Deloitte, Accenture and even General Electric, the company that popularised the idea initially.[143] Don't follow management trends dogmatically. Like any other part of your business, you should test your HR processes and learn what works for you. Who is to say what is "best practice"?

> *Processes make good servants but bad masters.*
>
> *~ Anon*

Summary

Key Points

- The source of many cultural problems in organisations is the management system used to strengthen individual's performance.
- At its worst, this manifests as a vitality curve or forced distribution.
- The approach is to rank individuals by their contribution and then apply incentives or punishments.
- There are problems with this approach, specifically:
  - It is not possible to rank individuals' performance accurately.
  - Telling people that they are poor performers will cause them to perform poorly (the Pygmalion Effect).
  - Individual contingent (if, then) incentives have unintended results.
- Individual performance has a limited impact on a business's performance.
- Team performance is more significant than individual performance.
- System performance is more significant than team performance.
- Perversely, the individuals who have the most effect on an organisation are the senior people. These people hand out the performance grades rather than receive them from below.
- Performance management programmes are a big opportunity cost.
- Bad performers stand out. They should be managed immediately rather than as part of an annual cycle.

Actions

- Collate employee feedback about the efficacy of your organisation's employee performance management process.
- List the desired outcomes of this process and the positive and negative results they create.
- Redesign and/or split the processes so that they give a better outcome.
- Test the revised processes, then learn and refine them accordingly.

Chapter 12:
A Thriving Culture

Killer Viruses, Wildfires, Aircraft Disasters and the World's Richest Men

Professor Jenkins (creator of The Performance Pyramid) claimed that a learning organisation has four critical cultural aspects:

- Constant communication.
- A no-blame philosophy.
- A long-term perspective.
- A one-team mindset.

His list may not be exhaustive, but it provides a thought-provoking place to start. Whilst these behaviours sound easy and obvious, they are much harder to pull off than you might think.

Listen Up

In the late noughties, Michelle Barton and Kathleen Sutcliffe studied firefighting teams in the US.[144] Some wildfires are well controlled and brought to a swift and safe conclusion, whilst others run havoc and cause millions of dollars of damage to thousands of acres of land. They wanted to understand how firefighters managed the complexity and hazards of their job, and discover what made them succeed or fail.

The researchers interviewed 28 firefighters from the western states and collated information from 62 different incidents. They categorised the outcome of the fires as good or bad by how well the firefighters managed to control the blaze. At one extreme, fires were quickly extinguished. At the other, they caused significant damage, and occasionally, firefighters had to run for their lives, literally.

Fire is mercurial. There are so many different aspects that can affect how it will develop:

- **Terrain and geography:** Is it hilly or flat?
- **Weather:** Is it hot or windy?
- **Undergrowth and vegetation:** Are they combustible?
- **Accessibility:** Can equipment be deployed?

All these individual factors change how fires behave. Once they start to interact with each other, conditions become hugely variable. Firefighting is the art of managing complexity. Barton and Sutcliffe's investigation showed patterns in the behaviour of those teams that controlled fires well and those that didn't.

The best firefighters were able to change their approach as the fire developed. They constantly re-evaluated conditions and modified their strategies. For them to do that, they had to have a deep understanding of the vagaries of the fire. Successful "Burn Bosses" could only achieve this if the lines of communication between them and their firefighters were open.

It wasn't enough to have regular, formal review sessions. A defined communication plan was invaluable, but the wind can always change direction seconds after a meeting. Nor was it enough to have an "open door" policy. Open doors are often guarded. The best fire chiefs actively sought disparate views from everyone around them. They would talk to their staff to understand how the fire was behaving at different locations.

Inherent within this approach was a healthy scepticism of experts. Whilst there is no substitute for experience, situational knowledge counts. Wise fire chiefs realised that if they only listened to the experts, others would hold back for fear of sounding stupid. Fear does nothing for open and honest voicing of worries and observations.

Fires don't suddenly flare out of control. There are always signs and clues that the intensity of a fire will change before it does. Successful firefighting relies on the constant flow of that knowledge. Strategies and approaches should change as the conditions do. As one fire chief put it:

> "(You have to) stimulate debate. You encourage it. And you don't enter in as a decision-maker. You don't start throwing your knowledge around. You don't want to say, well, I did so and so and such and such and blah, blah, blah because that just shuts them down. What you want is to encourage an open discussion of it among the technical experts, among the people who have knowledge. And if you can do that, it's amazing what you can find out."

The opposite behaviour was prevalent at the fires that got out of hand. The management teams were high-handed, didn't ask for opinions, kept themselves to themselves and called all the shots.

> "…they would have their get-togethers in a trailer, with just enough seats for them, you know, so nobody else could sit down…"

Those fire chiefs didn't have access to all the data, so they didn't adapt to changing circumstances. The managers didn't know best. The information was available, but their staff didn't share it. As it wasn't shared, it wasn't acted upon (unlike the Dutch electricity meters). On one occasion, a team was preparing to light a "controlled burn" to create a fire break. The fire escaped even though junior team members had noticed the adverse conditions; they didn't re-evaluate the situation.

"...it was really windy... we were sitting on the hoods of trucks. Actually sitting on one hood of a truck, looking at each other saying, 'hmm, kind of windy isn't it'..."

Culturally, there is nothing special about fighting fires. Barton and Sutcliffe's findings mirror what Pentland discovered with his communication badges. We all manage complexity in environments that we can't hope to understand. It doesn't matter if you are fighting fires, running a hospital or making toasters, situations change, and problems and issues arise.

Yet many managers don't seek out different perspectives and dissenting voices. Instead, they hold meetings with experts behind closed doors and dictate actions. An organisation that quashes dissent and enforces a "single narrative" will never have open and active communication. Poor outcomes are the price it will pay.

You Can Always Find a Fall Guy

On Sunday, the 1st of December 1974, Trans World Airlines (TWA) flight 514 flew towards Washington Dulles airport. As it came to land, the air traffic controller said, "Cleared for approach". The flight crew thought it meant one thing (we will guide you in), but the control tower meant something different (guide yourself in). It was a simple miscommunication.[145] TWA flight 514 flew straight into the side of Mount Weather, 510 meters above sea level. Ninety-two people died. There wasn't a single survivor because of a misunderstanding over a few words.

The Accident That Should Never Have Happened

You will know about the "Accident Triangle" if you have ever worked in health and safety. It is a simple idea:

1. For every fatal accident, there are a few serious accidents.
2. For every serious accident, there are several minor accidents.
3. For every minor accident, there are lots of near misses.

The causes of all these accidents (fatal, serious or minor) are the same, but the outcome rests on the circumstances. A toddler that chases a ball into the road could escape perfectly unharmed. It all depends on whether a juggernaut is approaching.

The Accident Triangle is closely related to the Swiss Cheese Effect that tragically led to Wayne Jowett's death in Nottingham's Queen's Medical Centre. As the number of minor incidents rises, the more likely it becomes that the holes will line up and there will be a severe accident. Consequently, health and safety professionals obsess about reducing near misses. Every time there is one, they insist it is reported and the cause removed. By removing the minor issues or "trips and slips", an organisation can reduce the chances of a fatality. H. W. Heinrich first put this idea forward in 1931.[146]

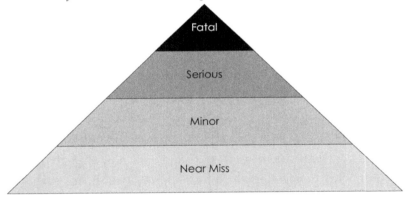

Figure 21: The Accident Triangle

The people responsible for US air safety in the 1970s, the Federal Aviation Administration (FAA), knew about Heinrich's triangle. They also knew exactly how to use it. They had mandated that aircrew report every near miss. It was the law, yet pilots routinely failed to highlight problems.

During the investigation into TWA flight 514, it became clear that this wasn't the first time a flight crew had misunderstood air traffic control's instructions. Six weeks earlier, a United Airlines flight had narrowly missed the same fate, brushing the treetops on the same hillside for the same reason. Yet the United Airlines flight pilots had kept quiet and ignored the law that they should have reported the incident.

It wasn't that the pilots didn't care about safety, just that they didn't trust the FAA. As well as collecting data on near misses and accident reporting, the FAA was also responsible for policing the aviation industry. They could fine, imprison and revoke the licences of pilots they caught doing wrong. This fact meant that a pilot had two options after a near miss. They could either speak up and risk losing their livelihood, or shut up and hope nobody else had the same misfortune. As the fear of being blamed for the incident outweighed the benefit of reporting it, many pilots and co-pilots chose the second option.

The National Aeronautics and Space Administration (NASA) came to the rescue and solved the problem. It took responsibility for collecting near-miss information and developed the Aviation Safety Reporting System (ASRS) that removed fear and blame. Pilots report incidents to NASA, but NASA cannot punish them. NASA then analyses the data and produces reports for the FAA, showing the high-risk areas. At the same time, they strip all the incriminating details from the information they have, and the pilots remain anonymous. As an additional incentive for pilots to report issues, it counts in their favour if the FAA ever investigates them, and they can show they reported an incident. The FAA sees this action as evidence of a "constructive safety attitude".[147] ASRS has a strapline that says it all:

"Confidential, Voluntary, Non-Punitive"

This approach is all very clever, but does the system work? Lina Connell, the scheme's director, celebrated its 40th anniversary in 2016, claiming that "Since the implementation of the Aviation

Safety Reporting System, approximately 1.4 million reports have been submitted by pilots, dispatchers, mechanics, air traffic controllers, flight attendants, ground personnel, and others."[148]

Over the same period, ASRS issued over 6,200 safety alerts to the FAA about numerous issues, from air traffic departure procedures to equipment problems and airport signs. Connell gave the example of a solar power plant in the southwestern United States reflecting intense sunlight and temporarily blinding pilots. Ultimately this led to cartographers marking the plant on aviation charts as a hazard. The information also changed how the operators used the plant, avoiding specific configurations of the solar panels.

Other enhancements included the "identification of fire hazards associated with the packaging of lithium-ion batteries for shipment in aircraft, health hazards associated with certain de-icing fluids, and the susceptibility of certain pressure-sensitive aircraft systems to icing from super-cooled water droplets."

The model has been copied worldwide. The International Confidential Aviation Safety Systems (ICASS) group helps member countries set up reporting systems. The United Kingdom runs the cheerfully named Confidential Human Factors Incident Reporting Program (CHIRP). Russia is not a member of ICASS. In 2016 The Sun newspaper ran the headline:

'IT WAS PILOT ERROR' First pictures of Russian plane crash pilot who the Kremlin 'blames' for deadly air disaster.[149] *

A Russian Defence Ministry jet had crashed into the Black Sea near Sochi, killing 92 people. After the crash, the Investigative

---

* The Sun is in the business of selling newspapers, not promoting aviation safety. Arguably, this is not true of the Kremlin. However, politicians worldwide have an unhelpful habit of making stupid inflammatory comments if they think it will win votes. Sadly, they are often right.

Committee of Russia launched a criminal case to probe the cause sending a clear message to pilots about accountability and the consequences of an accident.[150] I would be wrong to level responsibility for the disaster solely on Russia's approach to air safety reporting; the western world is far from perfect. Yet, coincidentally the Bureau of Aircraft Accidents Archives lists the Russian airline Aeroflot at the top of its list of civilian operators for all-time fatalities.*

It is worth remembering the words of the man who changed the culture at the Ford Motor Company and turned its fortunes around.

> *You have a problem; you are not the problem.*
>
> *~ Alan Mulally*

In a fair culture, people highlight issues. In organisations that apportion blame, people hide them.

> *Learn from the mistakes of others. You don't have time to make them all yourself.*
>
> *~ Eleanor Roosevelt*

Playing the Long Game

On Thursday, the 15th of May 1997, Amazon floated on the stock market. The company offered its shares for $18 each. Later that year, Jeff Bezos wrote his first letter to shareholders alongside Amazon's annual report. That letter was entitled "It's All About the Long-Term".[151] Mr Bezos wrote many things, but a few of the sentences stick out:

---

*Over the past century, flying with the RAF has been marginally more dangerous than flying with Aeroflot, but the statistics include multiple wars and the additional peril of being shot at.

"We believe that a fundamental measure of our success will be the shareholder value we create over the long-term...

Because of our emphasis on the long-term, we may make decisions and weigh trade-offs differently than some companies...

We will continue to make investment decisions in light of long-term market leadership considerations rather than short-term profitability considerations or short-term Wall Street reactions...

When forced to choose between optimizing the appearance of our GAAP accounting and maximizing the present value of future cash flows, we'll take the cash flows."

Mr Bezos claimed he would always guide the company to take the long-term view of opportunities rather than play a knee-jerk response to the financial markets. In an interview Bezos gave to Four Peaks TV, he defined the Amazon cocktail as a combination of customer centricity, long-term thinking and a passion for invention.[152] He then emphasised how well these things hang together:

"If you're going to invent, it means you're going to experiment, and if you're going to experiment, it means you are going to fail, and if you're going to fail, you'll have to think long-term."

In a separate interview given to Wired, Bezos spelt out the competitive advantage that taking the long-term perspective afforded Amazon.[153]

"If everything you do needs to work on a three-year time horizon, then you're competing against a lot of people. But if you're willing to invest on a seven-year time horizon, you're now competing against a fraction of those people, because very few companies are willing to do that. And just by lengthening the time horizon, you can engage in endeavors that you could never otherwise pursue. At Amazon, we like things to work in five to seven years. We're willing to plant seeds, let them grow."

In his seventh letter to Amazon shareholders, Bezos gave examples of some of the long-term decisions that Amazon had made:

"Shortly after launching Amazon.com in 1995, we empowered customers to review products. While now a routine Amazon.com practice, at the time we received complaints from a few vendors, basically wondering if we understood our business: 'You make money when you sell things—why would you allow negative reviews on your website?' Speaking as a focus group of one, I know I've sometimes changed my mind before making purchases on Amazon.com as a result of negative or lukewarm customer reviews. Though negative reviews cost us some sales in the short term, helping customers make better purchase decisions ultimately pays off for the company.

Another example is our Instant Order Update feature, which reminds you that you've already bought a particular item. Customers lead busy lives and cannot always remember if they've already purchased a particular item, say a DVD or CD they bought a year earlier. When we launched Instant Order Update, we were able to measure with statistical significance that the feature slightly reduced sales. Good for customers? Definitely. Good for shareowners? Yes, in the long run."[154]

Amazon is fearless in taking a long-term decision that will hurt its short-term profitability, knowing that the long game will prevail. If you had purchased one Amazon share in 1997 for $18, then today, via the financial wizardry of stock splits, you would have 240 shares. They are worth about $135 each, or $32,400 in total. Undoubtedly, there is more to that 180,000% return than simply building a culture that plays the long game, though it certainly didn't hurt.

Mr Bezos continues his fixation on the future. He has stepped down from his position as CEO at Amazon. He is currently busy at Blue Origin, where he is *"Building a road to space so our children can build the future."*

It Isn't Just Amazon

In 2009, Paul Polman became the chief executive of the Anglo-Dutch FMCG conglomerate Unilever. On his first day, he scrapped quarterly earnings reports saying:

> "Unilever has been around for 100-plus years. We want to be around for several hundred more … So if you buy into this long-term value-creation model, which is equitable, which is shared, which is sustainable, then come and invest with us. If you don't buy into this, I respect you as a human being, but don't put your money in our company."[155]

The billionaire investor Warren Buffett wrote in his 2019 letter to shareholders in his company Berkshire Hathaway:[156]

"Berkshire has no company-wide budget (though many of our subsidiaries find one useful). Our lack of such an instrument means that the parent company has never had a quarterly 'number' to hit. Shunning the use of this bogey sends an important message to our many managers, reinforcing the culture we prize.

Over the years, Charlie and I have seen all sorts of bad corporate behaviour, both accounting and operational, induced by the desire of management to meet Wall Street expectations. What starts as an 'innocent' fudge in order to not disappoint 'the Street' — say, trade-loading at quarter-end, turning a blind eye to rising insurance losses, or drawing down a 'cookie-jar' reserve— can become the first step toward full-fledged fraud. Playing with the numbers 'just this once' may well be the CEO's intent; it's seldom the end result. And if it's okay for the boss to cheat a little, it's easy for subordinates to rationalize similar behaviour."

If your organisation fixates on quarterly and annual targets, then it will make decisions that optimise short term profitability. Consequently, it will miss opportunities that its more farsighted competitors can take.

Together Everyone Achieves More

A "one-team" culture is an aspirational goal that few managers would disagree with. As we have discussed, the benefits of teamwork are numerous. Many hands make light work. The more people you can allocate to an initiative, the easier it will be to implement. Secondly, teamwork is the antithesis of the infighting that plagues many organisations, so one-team equals "no backstabbing" and more productive work. Finally, diversity fosters innovation. The greater the range of perspectives and experiences you can bring to a problem, the more likely you will overcome it. There is so much motherhood and apple pie associated with teamwork that it maxes out on the trite but true scale:

"There is no I in TEAM"

"TEAM = Together Everyone Achieves More"

Whilst the sentiment may leave you feeling slightly queasy, if an organisation genuinely invokes teamwork, it can achieve extraordinary things.

Eradicating Smallpox

Smallpox was an unpleasant disease.[157] People who contracted it developed a fever and started vomiting. This was followed by mouth ulcers and a skin rash that became characteristic, fluid-filled blisters with a dent in the middle. Eventually, these blisters scabbed over and fell off. The disease killed about 30% of those infected, whilst survivors had extensive scarring and, on many occasions, were left blind. If you run an online search for smallpox and look at the pictures, they are horrific.

During the 18th century, smallpox killed 400,000 Europeans every year. The disease was a plague of biblical proportions. The big preventative breakthrough came in 1796 when Edward Jenner, a doctor in rural Gloucestershire, noticed that inoculation with the related, but much less severe, cowpox virus provided immunity. This discovery started a vaccination drive (the term comes from the Latin word vaccinus, or "of the cow"). By the end of the 19th century, the number of cases had substantially reduced in North America and Europe. Yet, even by the mid-20th century, two million people died from the disease annually. In the late 1950s,

Professor Viktor Zhdanov, Deputy Minister of Health for the USSR, called for a global initiative to eradicate smallpox.

Only humans carried the disease, there wasn't a vector (like mosquitoes and malaria), so the strategy was to vaccinate every living human being and exterminate the virus. The plan, however, was far easier said than done. The problems that had to be overcome appeared to be insurmountable.

The first issue was resources. Only $100,000 per year was allocated to the task, so the WHO had to beg for vaccine doses, staffing and funds.[158] During the first few years, the USSR donated 140 million doses of the vaccine annually and the US a further 40 million. Twenty-four other countries also contributed, but as the quality was unknown, two centres in Canada and the Netherlands tested all the vaccines. Eventually, vaccine production was started in the countries where it was needed.

The original plan of 100% vaccination also proved impossible.[159] Geographical, religious, political and moral challenges made it an unachievable objective. The WHO moved to a more pragmatic and targeted detection and isolation strategy. The ill were quarantined whenever health workers identified an outbreak, and all their neighbours and contacts were vaccinated.

To enact this strategy, the WHO established a network of consultants who helped countries set up surveillance and containment activity. However, only 5% of outbreaks were reported. Some governments refused to admit they had a problem, leading to false claims of eradication by government decree. (Remember North Korea's reported Covid rates, and this isn't too hard to believe.) In India, the authorities overcame the problem by offering a 100-rupee reward (roughly £50 in 2023) to anybody who identified an outbreak. This strategy led to thousands of extraneous cases of chickenpox and scabies being reported and investigated.

The programme also received some significant geo-political setbacks. In Eritrea, the war of independence with Ethiopia became so violent that vaccination staff repeatedly withdrew from their work for fear for their lives. In 1970, Bangladesh was declared smallpox free, but by 1974 it harboured 90% of the world's smallpox as refugees returned to the country from camps in Kolkata (Calcutta).

The most graphic examples of the eradication team's challenges were at a personal level. Consultants in India customarily lost 4 to 10 kilos in weight over a three-month service period as the work was so arduous. When an outbreak was reported in Ethiopia, near the Sudanese border, a runner carried news of the disease on foot. He travelled for two days to the nearest police radio station. As the local airstrip was flooded, the surveillance officer who responded had to travel 315 miles to reach the affected region. The journey took him 15 days, and it turned out to be a false alarm caused by chickenpox.

Despite these difficulties, health workers diagnosed the last naturally occurring case of smallpox in Ali Maow Maalin, a hospital cook in Merca, Somalia, in 1977. Tragically, a year later, the final death from smallpox happened. A medical photographer, Janet Parker, caught the disease at the University of Birmingham Medical School and died. It is unclear how she became infected, but investigators showed that the source was a smallpox culture grown for research purposes at the medical school laboratory. Since then, all bar two cultures of smallpox have been destroyed. One remains in a research establishment in the United States, and another in Russia.

It is remarkable what people can achieve when they work as one-team.

The Fight Against Polio

Polio is also a very unpleasant disease, and it shares several characteristics with smallpox that make it technically feasible to eradicate. It is only found in humans, not in other animals, and it is treatable with both an oral and an injected vaccine. There is also a diagnostic tool available to identify the infection and allow track and trace activity.[160] Whilst many geopolitical factors still make the disease challenging to eradicate, these are the same as those that faced the people who battled smallpox, so they are not insurmountable.

In 1988, the WHO and the United Nations Children's Fund (UNICEF) took up the cause and steadfastly started eliminating the disease. The battle has been remarkably successful, yet as of today, in 2023 (35 years on), polio is still endemic in two countries, Afghanistan and Pakistan, so there is always a risk of an outbreak. This reality begs the question, why is the disease so hard to eradicate in those two countries?

There are several issues, but one of the biggest is a strong distrust of the US and its Western Allies. America's invasions of Iraq and Afghanistan have resulted in a profound scepticism of the west's motivations. Rumours have run amok in the Muslim world, with claims that the polio immunisation campaigns were used to sterilise Muslim populations or infect them with HIV.

As the saying goes, there is no smoke without fire. Following the 9/11 atrocities, the US Government tasked the Central Intelligence Agency (CIA) with finding and eliminating Osama bin Laden. They achieved their goal 10 years later in 2011 when a US task force entered Pakistan and killed bin Laden in his home in Abbottabad.

This US action on foreign soil resulted in a political uproar in Pakistan, and the Pakistani authorities held an enquiry into the Americans' activities in their country. Amongst other findings, the investigation uncovered an attempt by the CIA to confirm bin Laden's location.[161] The CIA had a genetic fingerprint of the bin Laden family, which they could use to identify relatives, particularly bin Laden's children. They organised a fake immunisation programme to collect blood samples from what they thought to be Osama bin Laden's compound in Abbottabad. The CIA had hoped to uncover bin Laden's presence by confirming the genetic identity of the children living there.

The subsequent media backlash was so damaging to the polio vaccination programme that an American association of some 200 US-based NGOs formally complained to the director of the CIA. In 2011, Pakistan reported the world's highest number of polio cases, and over 60 polio vaccination workers were killed between December 2012 and April 2014.

The point of this story is not to debate the political rights or wrongs of the US's interventions in the Middle East, but to show both the power and fragility of one-team cultures. Achieving true teamwork is possible if there is a clear unifying purpose. But even then, it is a mercurial achievement, no matter how noble your goal is.

The Cultural Roller Coaster

In April 1975, two childhood friends, Bill Gates and Paul Allen, set up a company to supply software for the Altair 8800 microcomputer. The friends called the company Micro-soft, short for microcomputer software.[162] Five years later, the company got a huge break when IBM awarded it the contract to supply an operating system, MS-DOS, for their personal computer.

Paul Allen resigned from Microsoft in 1983 after developing Hodgkin's lymphoma. Bill Gates went on to release Windows, a graphical extension of MS-DOS, and took the company on to become the world's biggest supplier of PC operating systems.

When the company went public in 1986, analysts estimated that the first stock offering created four billionaires and 12,000 millionaires among its employees.

In 1990, Microsoft introduced the Office suite, which bundled separate applications such as Word and Excel. Both Office and Windows became the dominant players in their segments. Microsoft cornered so much of the market that it became subject to investigations by the US Department of Justice's Antitrust Division.

Microsoft expanded its product line into computer networking and the world wide web. By December 2000, Microsoft had a market capitalisation of $510 billion, making it the world's most valuable company. Yet inside the organisation, all was not well.

In 2000, Bill Gates gave up his position as CEO, handing it over to a long-time friend and colleague, Steve Ballmer. Over the next 14 years, Microsoft lost the plot. Google and Facebook transformed the internet and social media, and Apple, which Microsoft employees had regarded as a basket case, stole consumers' hearts (and wallets). Microsoft had to resort to milking its old favourites, Windows and Office, to maintain its position. By 2012, Microsoft's market capitalisation had shrunk from $510 billion to $249 billion, whilst Apple had reached $541 billion. One Apple product, the iPhone, had greater sales values than all of Microsoft Corporation's products together.

The corporation had lost its innovative edge. In the late 1990s, Microsoft engineers, inspired by *The Hitchhiker's Guide to the Galaxy*, developed an e-book that worked with touchscreen technology, but senior managers shelved the project as it didn't fit with Windows. In 2001, Apple introduced its ubiquitous music player, the iPod. After five years, Microsoft released a "me too" product called Zune, only to watch Steve Jobs unveil the iPhone two months later. Zune flopped.

Google stole a march on web search, and in 2004, it floated on the stock exchange, creating a flood of millionaires, as Microsoft had done 18 years earlier. It wasn't until 2009 that Steve Ballmer unveiled Microsoft's search engine, Bing. Then, to add insult to injury, Google started eating Microsoft's breakfast by releasing Google Docs and Google Chrome OS, free software that targeted Microsoft Office and Windows.

In 2012, Vanity Fair published an article, *Microsoft's Lost Decade*.[163] Journalists interviewed Microsoft employees to understand why the organisation had lost its way. The company had hired many of the cleverest people in the world and had billions of dollars to throw at problems, yet it was losing ground to old and new competitors. The article claimed that at the heart of the problem was the organisation's culture.

Steve Ballmer had an aggressive and combative style, berating employees. When a senior software engineer handed in his notice to go and work for Eric Schmidt at Google, Ballmer erupted.

> "Fucking Eric Schmidt is a fucking pussy! ... I'm going to fucking bury that guy! I have done it before, and I will do it again. I'm going to fucking kill Google."

The aggression from the top pervaded Microsoft. The organisation became one where it was better not to stick your head above the parapet and try anything new or risky but instead manage the status quo. Bureaucracy and hierarchy flourished. As the early days of technical supremacy vanished, engineers realised that the chances of becoming wealthy through computing advances had also disappeared. Instead, the best way to get on was to get promoted, join the management hierarchy, and create meetings, memos and policies, not software. Tenured employees who had share options exacerbated the situation. These executives were happy to let newcomers do the work while waiting for their share options to mature. The casual attitude was scornfully known as "rest and vest" by new hires.

Many employees claimed that the core of Microsoft's problem was an internal "Stack Ranking" process. The system, a form of vitality curve or forced distribution, started in 1996.[164] A panel of managers ranked employees' performance, and then a forced distribution was applied to grade them. This system had a real-world impact on employees, resulting in large bonuses and promotions for the top-ranking employees, or contract termination for those at the bottom of the curve. According to Eichenwald, author of the Vanity Fair article:

> "Every current and former Microsoft employee I interviewed—every one— cited stack ranking as the most destructive process inside of Microsoft."

The process, with its simplistic logic, resulted in numerous unintended side effects. The primary issue was that it led to internal competition. As one executive said:

> "It leads to employees focusing on competing with each other rather than competing with other companies."

Another engineer admitted that:

> "People responsible for features will openly sabotage other people's efforts. One of the most valuable things I learned was to give the appearance of being courteous while withholding just enough information from colleagues to ensure they didn't get ahead of me on the rankings."

Yet another employee explained that the most talented engineers would do anything they could to avoid working alongside other capable people for fear of what it would do for their ranking.

Another side effect of the system is that it led to ruthless brown-nosing.

> "I was told in almost every review that the political game was always important for my career development … It was always much more on 'Let's work on the political game' than on improving my actual performance."

What you said became far more critical than what you did. The calibration sessions became much less about individuals' performance and more about their visibility. Calibrating managers would play games in the sessions, busily trying to protect their employees' positions. As the organisation removed its "lowest performing" employees every year, the competition in the review sessions became more brutal, and the games became more ruthless.

A third implication of the system was that managers held review sessions every six months. This frequency, of course, meant that everybody focused on short-term results rather than the bigger picture.

Morale and motivation dropped, so senior managers commissioned employee surveys to understand the cause of the company's problems. The feedback came back thick and fast; stack ranking was the source of much employee disillusionment. In response, in 2011, the chief executive doubled down on the programme, sending an email to all employees, making the programme more explicit.

"We are making this change, so all employees see a clear, simple, and predictable link between their performance, rating, and compensation."[165]

Some people complain that the Vanity Fair article overplayed the impact of stack ranking on Microsoft's performance. In contrast, one pair of Microsoft employees were so disillusioned they wrote a book about their experience.[166] *

In November 2013, Lisa Brummel, who led the HR function for the company, sent an e-mail to all Microsoft employees. The e-mail signalled the end of Microsoft's stack ranking process. It said there would be "no more curve" or "a pre-determined targeted distribution." Instead, teamwork and collaboration were to be prioritised in employee evaluations, which aligned with the organisation's "One Microsoft" philosophy.[167]

Steve Ballmer stepped down the following year, and Satya Nadella was named Microsoft's third CEO. Nadella is a different proposition to both Ballmer and Gates. He is undoubtedly a talented businessman, but also so calm that some describe him as beatific.[168]

Nadella played some very shrewd commercial moves. He purchased GitHub and LinkedIn (both have increased in value since their purchase) and offloaded the company's loss-making Nokia acquisition, believing smartphones were a lost cause for Microsoft. More subtly, he stopped using the term Windows, refocusing the organisation on artificial intelligence and the Azure cloud platform. He also turned Office into a software-as-a-service offering, even releasing the Office productivity suite on arch-rival Apple's iPhone.[169]

---

* The book doesn't get rave reviews. One reader believed it suffered from too much bold text, which is the literary equivalent of shouting. All the same, you'd have to be miffed to find the time to write a book about an ex-employer. I had six before I wrote this.

But perhaps the core of Nadella's success has been his belief that the "C" in CEO stands for culture and that, as the CEO, he is responsible for curating Microsoft's culture.[170] Nadella refuses to tolerate anger or yelling in executive meetings and has embraced the work of Carol Dweck of Stanford University, promoting what Dweck calls "a growth mindset". He has urged Microsoft's employees to change from its "know it all" view of the world to become a "learn it all" organisation focused on delivering Microsoft's vision of *"Empowering every person and every organisation on the planet to achieve more."*

Nadella has strived to change the behaviour within Microsoft, reducing political backbiting and bureaucracy and promoting learning, humility, acceptance of change and openness to external ideas. All of this has turned around Microsoft's fortunes. The company he inherited from Steve Ballmer in 2014 was worth $300 billion. At the end of 2021, it was worth two and a half trillion dollars and is busy battling it out with Apple as the world's most valuable company.

It is impossible to say how much of that financial turnaround is due to luck, strategy or culture. Yet, both current and ex-employees have given the company a Glassdoor (a recruitment and job website) approval rating of 95%. It is a very different place to the "rank and yank" Microsoft of old.

Summary
Key Points
- Culture underpins behaviour. It is the most potent determinant of organisational performance. To quote Peter Drucker (for a second time, but it is a strong point), "Culture eats strategy for breakfast."

- There are many ways to define a culture, but four elements that enable organisational learning (and hence improvement) are:
  - Constant communication.
  - A no-blame philosophy.
  - Taking a long-term perspective.
  - A one-team mindset.
- Some businesses have achieved this, but it takes continued focus from the top.
- It is easy to fall from grace and regress away from enlightened behaviour to our more caveman-like instincts.

Actions

- Evaluate your organisation against those four cultural dimensions (not the entire corporation, but the bit you are responsible for). An open and honest conversation with your team should give you plenty to work with.
- If you can't have an open conversation, that tells you what you need to know.
- Address the issues you discover.

Part 5.

The Choice

Chapter 13:
Don't Be a Moron

Which Way Will You Jump?

There is a vast market in management textbooks that seek out high-performing organisations and use them as beacons to show how to manage a business well. In my time, I have read *Good to Great, Built to Last,* and *In Search of Excellence.* Each of these books sold by the million as they provided a blueprint for good management practice. However, within a few years of publication, critics discredited the books as the companies they held up as exemplars failed.

In this book, I have singled out (amongst others) Microsoft, Amazon, IKEA and Whirlpool as examples of companies doing the right things. I am sure they have their failings. They have all had a healthy dose of luck, and no doubt they will falter somehow. The issue isn't what the organisations do but how their managers do it. Whilst one of the underlying messages in this book is that productivity is about the system and not the people, there is an exception. The people sitting at the organisation's very top have a disproportionate effect. They are the guardians of its culture. When those people move on, for better or worse, their organisation's performance will change. The Microsoft saga should convince you of that.

When I started my career, I was one of about 100 graduate management trainees. There was intense rivalry between us to see who would be promoted to a management grade first, and a belief that if you were "a good manager" you would climb the corporate ladder. Therefore logically, if you got promoted, you must be "good". Thirty-three years and six corporations on, I know that isn't true. Like everybody else, I have worked for a handful of fabulous bosses, had my share of fools, and suffered one or two who should have been taken outside and shot.* Seniority and management capability do not always go hand in hand.

The Executive Idiot

On Friday, the 31st of March 2023, millions of school children in the UK broke up for their Easter break. Some were lucky enough to board a coach that afternoon and head off to the Alps for their school's annual skiing trip. A week of snow, blue skies, flirting with their classmates, and general fooling about lay before them. It is most teenagers' dream holiday.

At 11 o'clock that evening, the Port of Dover, from where the ferries depart to Calais in northern France, declared a state of emergency. They had been inundated with hundreds of coaches and couldn't deal with them all. A line of buses and schoolchildren trailed back up the main A2 trunk road towards London.

One frustrated coach driver, carrying nearly 50 children from South Wales to the Italian Alps, complained that some of his children had been physically sick and had not eaten for 15 hours. He added, "The only facilities the coaches and children had access to was a small petrol station, which due to the capacity of people, couldn't cope... There wasn't enough food, and the toilets ran out of toilet paper."[171]

The Twittersphere was also alive with complaints. One parent claimed that his children's coach had arrived at the port at 10:30 that morning and hadn't managed to get through passport control

---

*That isn't politically correct of me, but maybe you have also worked for them and can sympathise.

until nearly 12 hours later.[172] Another wag posted a picture of the British Prime Minister, Rishi Sunak, asking a coach passenger, "Would you mind getting off and swimming? It's only 27 miles, and the tide's out."[173] Fortunately, within a day or so, the port cleared the backlog, and the ferry traffic returned to normal. It wasn't serious, nobody died, but nobody had much fun.

Later that weekend, the UK Home Secretary, Suella Braverman, was asked on a news programme if the UK's withdrawal from the European Union (EU) was responsible for the delays. She denied this, stating, "No, I don't think that's fair to say that this has been an adverse effect of Brexit." In a subsequent interview, she blamed "bad weather" and "a particular combination of factors" and said that it was "ultimately an issue for the ferry companies".[174] The port authorities saw the situation differently, saying the delays were "due to lengthy French border processes and sheer volume".[175]

The trigger for the headlines and angst was a simple operational reality. One of the last things to happen at Dover before vehicles are allowed onto a ferry is that they must pass through French passport control. Every morning, a team of immigration officers commutes across the channel from Calais to Dover, where they man the first bastion of EU bureaucracy, a set of immigration booths.

Having this check before passengers board a ferry makes more sense as it speeds unloading at the other end of the crossing. Before the UK left the EU in 2020, UK citizens were entitled to move freely across Europe, so immigration was little more than a cursory check to ensure nobody had two heads or was carrying a machine gun. Now, however, the immigration officer must check the person matches the passport and then date stamp and record it. Whilst this is only a slight extra delay for the lone driver of a car, it represents a significant impediment to the movement of coaches as the identity of every single passenger must be verified and recorded.

This particular disaster was not unforeseen. Hundreds of extra coaches had booked and paid for their crossings in advance. It was no surprise when they arrived. Anybody with a stopwatch and a calculator could have counted the passport booths, timed how long it took to process a coach and worked out how big the tailback and delay would become. I'd wager my mortgage that that is what the port authorities had done.

However, the bottleneck in the process was crossing the French border. This stage was totally outside the control of the port and shipping authorities, and ultimately it was the responsibility of the UK Home Secretary to agree with her French counterparts. Unfortunately, this practical reality didn't play well to the political rhetoric, and the politicians and civil servants ignored the warning signs. Is it a surprise that the spokesman for the port admitted that he was "deeply frustrated"?

A Three-Way Choice

This story isn't about Brexit or party politics.* Brexit does however make a point about office politics beautifully. Of those who voted in the 2016 referendum, 48.1% wanted to stay in the Union, whereas 51.9% voted to leave. The UK's exit from the European Union has continued to be a hot topic in pubs and living rooms ever since. If you voted in the referendum, this story might have provoked a gut reaction. You might deny that your vote had anything to do with the issue, or you may be smugly nodding in agreement, happily thinking "I told you so" to yourself. Neither response would have helped the stranded children.

When something goes awry, managers have a three-way

---

*Delays at Dover are a tiny side effect of Brexit. It will be decades before historians have can say whether the decision was a success, and even then, we will continue to argue.

choice. They can either dismiss the situation, point score and make political capital, or face and fix the problem. Suella Braverman is a powerful lady. She could have admitted there were issues and asked one of her team to work with the French to increase capacity or throughput at the border. Instead, she blamed "bad weather" and refuted the reality. It was politically expedient to do so. I do not doubt that if the situation was reversed and the UK had voted to remain, some other politician would be sitting there denying that another issue (straight bananas or dodgy sausages) was caused by a decision to stay.

We are humans, not the ultra-logical Vulcans of Star Trek fame; politics and diplomacy are part of our nature, but they can be overplayed. There are managers at all levels who are busier concocting stories than solving problems. They stick their head in the sand, blame others, sit in judgement and manage the message, all to look good. They are morons, but nobody says you must join them. If you want your organisation to thrive, all you need do is:

1. Create a clear direction.
2. Listen to your teams.
3. Fix the issues that get in your way.

It is that simple. If you follow the steps, gradually building capability as you go, you can't help but succeed, and your teams and customers will love you for it. You and your organisation will stand head and shoulders above other "managers" who are busily spinning stories.

You can't avoid fools and corporate clones, but you can make your organisation thrive. Life is too short to be another management moron.

God grant me the serenity to accept the things I cannot change, courage to change the things I can, and the wisdom to know the difference.

~ Winnifred Crane Wygal

Part 6.

Extras

Recap

If you are anything like me, you can read a book and instantly forget it; it will go in one ear and out of the other (that is either biological gibberish or an audiobook). Here is a recap to help you remember what you have just read or to tear out and give to someone with a short attention span. Creating a thriving organisation is straightforward. Here are the steps to follow.

Stage 1. Create Focus

First, **clarify purpose.** What do you want to thrive at? Nobody enjoys pointless work. That purpose must be externally focused and engaging. If it is self-serving, your organisation will run out of customers and if it is boring, it will run out of employees. Only the desperate or disillusioned want boring work.

Then, **measure performance against that purpose.** Are you achieving it? People engage with activities when they can see how they are doing. They like to know the score. If they don't know how they are progressing, they will soon become uninterested and give up.

Stage 2. Promote Learning

The next step is to **concentrate your efforts on improving your systems.** There are two ways to develop an organisation, get better people and build better systems (business processes, information technology, conveyor belts, routing patterns, schedules, the way work is done). Sports teams compete by training and hiring the best people, but they hardly improve; they run hard to stand still. The ten-second barrier for the 100-meter sprint was first broken in 1968. Fifty-five years on, the record stands at 9.58 seconds. In half a century, speed has increased by less than 5%. Systems have, however, come on in leaps and bounds. In 1968, man hadn't stepped foot on the moon, and now we have TikTok. (Maybe not the most compelling example, but you understand my point). Running a business isn't the same as running a sports team. Yes, you should train and develop your people, but the leverage is in building better systems. Innate human performance doesn't change much. Processes and systems do.

Step four is to **engage your teams**. Our organisations are complicated. Even a one-man gardener relies on a lawn mower made in China, weed killer from a Swiss chemical plant and seed grown in Denmark. (Often a mix of dwarf ryegrass, slender creeping red fescue and bent grass. Who knew grass seed was so complicated?) Nobody can know and understand everything. To enhance your systems, you must rely on your workforce, as they are the people who understand them well enough to suggest how to develop them.

> *The lower the rank of managers, the more they know about fewer things. The higher the rank of managers, the less they know about many things.*
>
> *Russell L. Ackoff*

The fifth thing to do is to **test improvements**. Even your most knowledgeable staff don't know precisely how your systems work, there are scores of unforeseen interactions and side effects. The only way to enhance your systems is to test ideas and see what happens. Tests involve failure. If you know something won't fail, then it isn't a test and you won't learn from it. It is only possible to improve by testing, failing and learning.

Stage 3. Curate Culture

Finally (and this is the hard part), you must **create an environment where everybody can do their best work**. Somewhere they can work together to test, learn and improve. If you blame people for failure, they won't test anything new. If you set individual performance targets, they won't work as a team. If you focus on the short-term, you will miss out on the long-term opportunities. If you don't share knowledge, nobody can build on it.

If you strut about like an alpha male (or female), telling your staff what to do and slapping them when they step out of line, they will do exactly what you have asked of them. If you believe you are perfect, know everything, are never wrong, have a brain the size of the planet and the charisma to match, this is the best strategy. But you had better be sure. A slap in the face never motivated anybody to do anything but slap back. **Don't be a moron**.

The Summary of Summaries

For those with very short attention spans: or who are under intense pressure from their boss to do something (anything) right now.

1. Clarify purpose.
2. Measure progress.
3. Focus on systems.
4. Engage your teams.
5. Test improvements.
6. Create an environment where everybody can do their best work.
7. Don't be a moron.

Key Points and Actions

Here are all the points made throughout the book, the whole nine yards. Perhaps I should have put it at the front but that would have been cheating. You would never have made it to the end.

Break The Management Patterns

Most importantly, you must break the management patterns that stifle learning, engagement, and productivity improvement. Those patterns include:

- Commanding and controlling staff.
- Managing by targets rather than setting a direction.
- Intimidation and casting blame rather than seeking to understand the issues.
- Dictating action rather than listening to opinions.
- Burying failures rather than fessing-up.

Instead of managing people, you must manage culture and create an environment where your staff can do their best work.

Focus

Define Your Purpose

- Organisation is the art of coordinating effort. Write down what you want that coordinated effort to achieve.
- Focus on something external. Organisations exist to do something for somebody. If they lose sight of their customers, they strive to become efficient rather than effective. As Peter Drucker said: "There is nothing so useless as doing efficiently that which should not be done at all."

- Make your purpose statement memorable and engaging, not just management fluff. You will never excel if your aims are mediocre.
- Use your purpose statement as a standard against which to check your actions. If it is just words, it is worse than meaningless.

Build Measures

- You can only get better if you use measures to assess progress against your purpose.
- Do not obsess about creating perfect measures; measures are only a proxy for performance. It is far better to be approximately right rather than precisely wrong.
- Use measures to understand the reasons for variations in performance.
- You should use those measures to guide improvement, not control people.
- Remember, the minute a measure becomes a target, it becomes useless as a measure.

Learning

- Fess-up. You can only get better if you admit you have a problem.
- Visit the places where your organisation works. You won't find customers or enlightenment at head office.
- Share information and solicit input from your colleagues, team and outsiders. You do not have a moratorium on good ideas.
- Experiment. Run trials and tests to improve the way you operate.
- Measure the success of your trials. Without measuring the effect of a change, you can't tell if it improves things.
- If a trial works, roll it out. If it doesn't, back it out.

- Accept failure. Learning comes from failure (just make sure you have many small rather than a few big ones).
- Design and develop mechanisms to lock learning in.
- Be relentless. If your improvements aren't working, try something else, but never stop trying.

Culture

- Communicate openly, regularly, and freely.
- Remove fear. If your HR processes or managers scare your staff, change your HR processes or your managers.
- Remove blame. Performance is in the system, not the people. Instead of asking, "**Who** caused that?" understand, "**What** caused that?"
- Play the long game.
- Remove the barriers to teamwork.

And Finally

- Enable your staff. Provide direction, support and resources, then let them manage themselves.
- Humans make mistakes, they always have, and they always will.
- Build system capability.
- People cheat; don't give them a reason to.
- If your manager is a self-seeking moron, find a better one. Some people aren't worthy of your time.

Case Study

This book has plenty of examples of organisations that have messed things up. Disasters make good reading, and learning from failure is easier than success. I am still looking for a newspaper that has built its circulation on good news stories.

However, sometimes an example of what did work helps. Saying something and doing it are different things, and why am I sure what I propose will solve your organisational ills? The answer is that I have seen it work countless times in call centres, recruitment operations, sales forces, finance offices, legal teams and technology functions. Let me tell you about the first time.

The Hospital Pass

At one stage in my career, I received what is colloquially known as a "hospital pass"; somebody threw me a ball, knowing full well I would get trampled catching it. An executive far more senior than I had decided to combine an organisation's pockets of management information and analysis. They parcelled it all up and gave it to me so that I could create "efficiencies".

Twenty-seven people were rammed together into a new team that provided hundreds of reports to the business every month, ranging from daily call centre statistics to annual risk predictions. There was also an ongoing demand for new information to help the rest of the company explain what was happening.

Within about half an hour of an announcement that explained that I had received this "golden opportunity", the telephone started ringing. Every organisational baron and duke picked up the phone to tell me how important they were, that their teams depended on the information reaching them, and that the whole thing was chaos. The information the team provided was either late or wrong or (frequently) both. It was a blood bath (as close to slaughter as possible in a well-appointed office block that followed good health and safety practices). We had to be infinitely more productive.

Focus

First, we clarified the team's purpose. We concocted something suitably corporate: *"To deliver timely, accurate business insight."* It maybe wasn't as compelling as Google's mission statement, but it was customer-focused and a start.

Next, we turned our attention to measures, and I asked the team to tell me how timely and accurate their reports or insights were. I wanted a measure that showed how often the reports and ad-hoc requests were "On Time and In Full" (OTIF). Interestingly, the Management Information Department didn't have any management information.

The team regarded my request with horror. They didn't have a system to record their work. They were clear that if they were going to have a target, they needed a fully functional infrastructure to record the information correctly. Otherwise, it wouldn't be accurate, and people would be penalised unfairly. I explained that this wasn't a target and that I just needed a consistent measure to see if we were getting better and, if not, what was getting in the way. A daily five-bar gate (tally chart) would do, with everybody recording how they got on.

There was a lot of grumbling, but eventually, I got my measure, and our self-reported service levels were 99.99%. Yet the phone calls, complaints, bitching and moaning from the organisation's directors, vice presidents, and the occasional dictator kept coming. The team was lying to me through its teeth, our service was dreadful, but no one wanted to admit it for fear of what I would do. It took me three months to persuade them that I wouldn't jump up and down on their heads if our offering was poor. I just needed to know where the problems were so we could fix them.

Learning

Eventually, the team started to trust me and showed me the horror of the infrastructure they had to cope with in all its gory detail. Systems didn't talk to each other, software was unsupported, batches ran late, data tables were undocumented, and servers were so old they were cutting-edge during the moon shots of the 1960s. You didn't have to be a techno-nerd to understand how broken it was.

We then ran some "Work-Out" sessions, or what is now unfashionably known as "Quality Circles", and the teams told me what they needed help fixing.[176] I don't know anything about database schemas, extract, transform and load (ETL) or structured query language (SQL), but fortunately they did. They ran trial solutions, learnt what worked, and systematically addressed their most significant issues and problems.

Culture

For three years, we kept at it, with weekly reviews as I traipsed around the less glamorous corners of the organisation, visiting the various technological outposts everywhere from the balmy south coast to the frozen north (frequently passing through East Croydon). Every week or so, the team would fix, rewrite or stop doing something, always building capability.

We didn't build a "Target Operating Model" or have a grand plan. Our strategy was to **"Fix Stuff That Doesn't Work"**. Now and again, we had an issue and slipped backwards, but when that happened, we avoided recriminations. There was no need for a big song and dance. Everybody chipped in, and we kept on mending things.

The Proof Is in the Pudding

During that period, we measured performance to see if we were getting any better and if our customers were getting happier. We did this in four ways:

- The lead time to fulfil a new request (days).
- Customer satisfaction (an external NPS survey).[177]
- Cost to serve (team size).
- Employee satisfaction (an internal NPS survey).

It worked:

- Lead times dropped from an average of 20 days to less than two days (including weekends).
- Customer satisfaction rose from an NPS Score of -18 to +72. And the phone stopped ringing.
- Costs fell by 63% from 27 full-time equivalents to 10. Nobody was sacked (how can you expect people to give you their good ideas and implement them if you fire them afterwards?) Headcount drifted downwards due to natural attrition. The rest of the business respected the team, and members went on to bigger and better things.
- Employee satisfaction was the best bit. It rose from five to 65 points. No more "Monday morning blues".

It isn't a particularly dramatic story. We decided what we wanted to be, worked together, fixed the broken things, and had a ball doing it. Yet our results were outstanding. As the Americans would say, "Go Figure!" That is what thriving looks like. You should try it. It feels great.

Further Reading

They say everybody has a book inside them. I didn't; I had a copy and paste inside me. I rearranged some ideas I had read and heard elsewhere and joined a dot or two. This reading list should keep you occupied if you want to go to the original sources.

Adapt: Why Success Always Starts With Failure — Tim Harford.

"Tim Harford shows how the world's most complex and important problems — including terrorism, climate change, poverty, innovation, and the financial crisis — can only be solved from the bottom up by rapid experimenting and adapting."

Black Box Thinking: The Surprising Truth About Success — Matthew Syed.

"Black Box Thinkers see failure as the very best way to learn. Rather than denying their mistakes, blaming others, or attempting to spin their way out of trouble, these institutions and individuals interrogate errors as part of their future strategy for success."

The Checklist Manifesto: How to Get Things Right — Atul Gawande.

"We live in a world of great and increasing complexity, where even the most expert professionals struggle to master the tasks they face. Longer training, ever more advanced technologies — neither seems to prevent grievous errors. But in a hopeful turn, acclaimed surgeon and writer Atul Gawande finds a remedy in the humblest and simplest of techniques: the checklist."

The Design of Everyday Things — Donald A. Norman.

"The Design of Everyday Things shows that good, usable design is possible. The rules are simple: make things visible, exploit natural relationships that couple function and control, and make intelligent use of constraints. The goal: guide the user effortlessly to the right action on the right control at the right time."

Drive: The Surprising Truth About What Motivates Us — Daniel H. Pink.

"Drawing on four decades of scientific research on human motivation, Pink exposes the mismatch between what science knows and what business does — and how that affects every aspect of our lives. He demonstrates that while the old-fashioned carrot-and-stick approach worked successfully in the 20th century, it's precisely the wrong way to motivate people for today's challenges."

The Human Factor: Revolutionizing the Way People Live with Technology — Kim J. Vicente.

"Vicente makes vividly clear how we can bridge the widening gap between people and technology. He investigates every level of human activity — from simple matters such as our hand-eye coordination to complex human systems such as government regulatory agencies, and why businesses would benefit from making consumer goods easier to use."

Just Culture: Balancing Safety and Accountability — Sidney Dekker.

"How justice is created inside organizations. The goal remains the same: to create an environment where learning and accountability are fairly and constructively balanced."

The Leader's Handbook: Making Things Happen, Getting Things Done — Peter R. Scholtes.

"Scholtes shows how bad systems, not bad workers, cause the vast majority of management problems. He takes controversial stands against performance appraisals and incentive compensation and he takes you from theory to practice with a wide variety of state-of-the-art activities."

Meltdown: Why Our Systems Fail and What We Can Do About It — Chris Clearfield and András Tilcsik.

"World-leading experts in disaster prevention, Chris Clearfield and András Tilcsik, use real-life examples to reveal the errors in thinking, perception, and system design that lie behind both our everyday errors and disasters like the Fukushima nuclear accident."

Narconomics: How to Run a Drug Cartel — Tom Wainwright.

"How does a budding cartel boss succeed (and survive) in the $300 billion illegal drug business? By learning from the best, of course. From creating brand value to fine-tuning customer service, the folks running cartels have been attentive students of the strategy and tactics used by corporations such as Walmart, McDonald's, and Coca-Cola."

Pygmalion in Management: Harvard Business Review Classics — J. Sterling Livingston.

> "Numerous studies show that people will rise, or fall, to the level where their superiors believe them capable. As a manager, it is up to you to have high expectations for your employees, and to communicate those expectations to them. In Pygmalion in Management, J. Sterling Livingston urges you to understand the power you have over your subordinates' success, and use it to benefit everyone involved."

Seeing the Forest for the Trees: A Manager's Guide to Applying Systems Thinking — Dennis Sherwood.

> "Only by taking a broad view can we avoid the twin dangers of a silo mentality — in which a fix 'here' simply shifts the problem to 'there', and organisational myopia — in which a fix 'now' gives rise to a much bigger problem to fix 'then'."

Thinking in Systems: A Primer — Donella H. Meadows.

> "Some of the biggest problems facing the world — war, hunger, poverty, and environmental degradation — are essentially system failures. They cannot be solved by fixing one piece in isolation from the others, because even seemingly minor details have enormous power to undermine the best efforts of too-narrow thinking."

The Tiger That Isn't: Seeing Through a World of Numbers — Andrew Dilnot and Michael Blastland.

"Politicians, journalists and everyone in power use numbers all the time to bamboozle us. Most maths is really simple — as easy as 2+2 in fact. Better still, it can be understood without any jargon, any formulas — and in fact, not even many numbers. Most of it is common sense, and by using a few really simple principles, one can quickly see when maths, statistics and numbers are being abused to play tricks — or create policies — which can waste millions of pounds."

About the Author

James Lawther spent 33 years in corporate Britain. He has packed frozen peas, processed credit card applications, keyed in data, and paid insurance claims. He has stacked the nation's shelves with ready-made curry, sent the bailiffs around to collect taxes and made hundreds of thousands of tons of sweets. He finished his corporate career with the rather distinguished job title of Director of Data Operations. Whilst that sounds grand, it should be noted that job title inflation has been rampant over the past thirty years and a director isn't what it used to be. Besides, the acronym for the post was the dodo, a harsh but apt epithet.

As you can see from his CV, he either has a wealth of experience or cannot hold down a job.

During that time, he has tried to make the organisations work better, riling against the stupidity of others and cursing his political naivety. Whilst he was never called an executive idiot (at least not to his face), he was described in a year-end appraisal as the management equivalent of Marmite. (If you aren't British, you will have to search for the adverts on YouTube to understand.)

If you have got this far in the book, he hopes it gave you something to ponder, generated a wry smile, and he'd be very grateful if you left a review on Amazon or Goodreads to let him and others know what you thought.

Finally, if you want to thrive, he'd love to help. Drop him a line at james.lawther@squawkpoint.com.

Notes

1 **Bad Bosses** [Online] / auth. Adams Scott // Dilbert. - 06 November 2010. - https://dilbert.com/strip/2010-11-06.

2 **Tombstone** [Book] / auth. Jisheng Yang. - [s.l.] : Farrar Straus & Giroux, 2008.

3 **Tso-hsin Cheng** [Online] / auth. Wikipedia // Wikipedia. - https://en.wikipedia.org/wiki/Tso-hsin_Cheng

4 **The Hungry Years** [Online] / auth. Mishra Pankaj // The New Yorker. - 12 December 2012. - https://www.newyorker.com/magazine/2012/12/10/the-hungry-years.

5 **Exterminate the four pests!** [Online] / auth. Hao Ding // Chinese Posters. - January 1958. - https://chineseposters.net/posters/pc-1958-025.

"From 1956 onwards, mice, sparrows, flies, and mosquitoes should absolutely be eliminated in all possible places within 12 years. Killing sparrows serves to protect crops. Sparrows in cities and forest areas do not necessarily have to be eliminated."

6 **Great Chinese Famine** [Online] / auth. Wikipedia // Wikipedia. - https://en.wikipedia.org/wiki/Great_Chinese_Famine.

7 **Four Pests campaign** [Online] / auth. Wikipedia //. Wikipedia. - https://en.wikipedia.org/wiki/Four_Pests_campaign.

8 In 1998, Li Chengrui, former minister of the National Bureau of Statistics of China estimated 22 million deaths.

9 **Mao's Great Famine: The History of China's Most Devastating Catastrophe, 1958–62** [Book] / auth. Dikotter Frank. - [s.l.] : Walker & Company, 2010.

10 **Which Is Most Important, Perception or Performance?** [Online] / auth. Lawther James // Squawk Point. - April 2019. - https://www.squawkpoint.com/2019/04/perceived-performance/.

11 **999 Cars Bid to 'Fix Targets'** [Online] / auth. McDermott Nick // The Sun. - July 13, 2017. - https://www.thesun.co.uk/living/4006923/nhs-bosses-sending-cars-instead-of-ambulances-in-bid-to-fiddle-999-figures/.

12 **'Life-saving' cycle paramedics back on the road with new recruits on board** [Online] / auth. Place Clarissa // Eastern Daily Press. - 26 August 2020. - https://www.edp24.co.uk/news/health/20750886.life-saving-cycle-paramedics-back-road-new-recruits-board/.

13 **Red Bead Experiment with Dr. W. Edwards Deming** [Online] / auth. Hunter John // The W. Edwards Deming Institute. - 25 February 2014. - https://deming.org/deming-red-bead-experiment/.

14 **There's no putting on the brakes: Why businesses must learn to harness the power of change** [Online] / auth. Jenkins Mark // Cranfield School of Management. - May 23, 2018. - https://www.cranfield.ac.uk/som/thought-leadership-list/there-s-no-putting-on-the-brakes-why-businesses-must-learn-to-harness-the-power-of-change.

15 **About B&N** [Online] / auth. Barnes & Noble // Barnes & Noble. - 2022. - https://www.barnesandnobleinc.com/about-bn/.

16 **Our Mission** [Online] / auth. Amazon // Amazon. - April 18, 2018. - https://www.aboutamazon.co.uk/news/job-creation-and-investment/our-mission.

[17] **Unilever Sustainable Living Plan** [Online] / auth. Unilever // Unilever.com. - 2016. - https://assets.unilever.com/files/92ui5egz/production/ 716e32898ad8f69248f6f56bb47909fdfb937608.pdf/make-sustainable-living-commonplace-2016.pdf.

[18] **Strategy and Purpose** [Online] / auth. Lloyds Banking Group // Lloyds Banking Group. - https://www.lloydsbankinggroup.com/who-we-are/our-strategy.html.

[19] **Helping Britain Recover** [Online] / auth. Lloyds Banking Group // Lloyds Banking Group. - 2020. - https://www.lloydsbankinggroup.com/assets/pdfs/who-we-are/ responsible-business/helping-britain-prosper/2020/lbg-hbr-onepager-final-210223.pdf.

[20] **About Philips** [Online] / auth. Philips // Philips. - https://www.philips.com/a-w/about.html.

[21] **Our guiding principles** [Online] / auth. Exxon Mobil // Exxon Mobil. - 2018. - https:/ /corporate.exxonmobil.com/About-us/Who-we-are/Our-guiding-principles.

[22] **Ingvar Kamprad & family** [Online] / auth. Forbes // Forbes. - 2018. - https://www. forbes.com/profile/ingvar-kamprad/?sh=2004ee9417f4.

[23] **House Perfect** [Online] / auth. Collins Lauren // The New Yorker. - 26 September 2011. - https://www.newyorker.com/magazine/2011/10/03/house-perfect.

[24] **The IKEA vision and values** [Online] / auth. Kamprad Ingvar // IKEA. - https:// www.ikea.com/gb/en/this-is-ikea/about-us/the-ikea-vision-and-values-pub9aa779d0.

[25] **Fifty Things that Made the Modern Economy** [Book] / auth. Harford Tim. - [s.l.] : Abacus, 2018.

[26] **The Single Most Important Object in the Global Economy** [Online] / auth. Vanderbilt Tom // Slate. - 14 August 2012. - https://slate.com/business/2012/08/pallets-the-single-most-important-object-in-the-global-economy.html.

[27] **The Why, What, and How of Management Innovation** [Article] / auth. Hamel Gary // Harvard Business Review. - February 2006.

[28] **Innovation 101: Whirlpool's Spin on Innovation** [Online] / auth. Roosen Peter P. and Nakagawa Tatsuya // Industry Week. - 14 July 2008. - https://www.industryweek. com/leadership/companies-executives/article/21933039/innovation-101-whirlpools-spin-on-innovation.

[29] **A Strategy for Nottinghamshire's Libraries** [Online] / auth. Nottinghamshire County Council // Nottinghamshire County Council. - https://www.nottinghamshire. gov.uk/DMS/Document.ashx? czJKcaeAi5tUFL1DTL2UE4zNRBcoShgo=coVLl53FajEkjNl97fJz49N1P7b42Tz3kkcpH m1RoWIRXTU1WrqNQQ%3D%3D&rUzwRPf%2BZ3zd4E7Ikn8Lyw%3D%3D=pwRE 6AGJFLDNlh225F5QMaQWCtPHwdhUfCZ%2FLUQzgA2uL5jNRG4jdQ%3D%3D& mCTIbCubSFfXsD.

[30] **Systems Thinking** [Online] / auth. Wikipedia // Wikipedia. - https://en.wikipedia. org/wiki/Systems_thinking.

[31] **If Russ Ackoff Had Given a TED Talk** [Online] / auth. Ackoff Russell L. // YouTube. - 1994. - https://www.youtube.com/watch?v=OqEeIG8aPPk.

[32] **Differences between 20/20 cricket and Test cricket** [Online] / auth. Stack Exchange // Stack Exchange. - 17 August 2017. - https://sports.stackexchange.com/ questions/4287/differences-between-20-20-cricket-and-test-cricket.

[33] **Optimizing Each Part of a Firm Doesn't Optimize the Whole Firm** [Online] / auth. Satell Greg // Harvard Business Review. - 27 January 2016. - https://hbr.org/2016/01/ optimizing-each-part-of-a-firm-doesnt-optimize-the-whole-firm.

[34] **Team of Teams: New Rules of Engagement for a Complex World** [Book] / auth. McChrystal Stanley A. [et al.]. - [s.l.] : Penguin, 2015.

[35] **Our Approach to Search** [Online] / auth. Google // Google. - https://www.google.com/intl/en_uk/search/howsearchworks/our-approach/.

[36] **Wikimedia Foundation Mission** [Online] / auth. Wikimedia Foundation // Wikimedia Foundation. - https://wikimediafoundation.org/about/mission/.

[37] **Stories move us. They make us feel more emotion, see new perspectives, and bring us closer to each other.** [Online] / auth. Netflix // Netflix. - https://about.netflix.com/en.

[38] **Management: Tasks, Responsibilities, Practices** [Book] / auth. Drucker Peter F.. - [s.l.] : Harper & Row, 1974.

[39] **Do You Do Things Right, or Do the Right Things?** [Article] / auth. Drucker Peter F. // The Financial Post. - 6 March 1965. - p. 7.

[40] **Managing for Business Effectiveness** [Article] / auth. Drucker Peter F. // Harvard Business Review. - May 1963.

[41] **Purpose: Shifting from why to how** [Online] / auth. Gast Arne [et al.] // McKinsey & Company. - 22 April 2020. - https://www.mckinsey.com/business-functions/people-and-organizational-performance/our-insights/purpose-shifting-from-why-to-how.

[42] **Sears to Repair Image With $46 Million in Coupons** [Online] / auth. Gellene Denise // Los Angeles Times. - 3 September 1992. - https://www.latimes.com/archives/la-xpm-1992-09-03-fi-7430-story.html.

[43] **Should Companies Serve Only Their Shareholders Or Their Stakeholders More Broadly?** [Online] / auth. Pontefract Dan // Forbes. - 09 May 2016. - https://www.forbes.com/sites/danpontefract/2016/05/09/shareholders-or-stakeholders/.

[44] **How Dean Foods' bankruptcy is a 'warning sign' to the milk industry** [Online] / auth. Byington Lillianna // Food Dive. - November 21 2019. - https://www.fooddive.com/news/how-dean-foods-bankruptcy-is-a-warning-sign-to-the-milk-industry/.

[45] **About Southwest Airlines** [Online] // Southwest. - https://www.southwest.com/about-southwest/.

[46] **Problems of Monetary Management: The UK Experience** [Book Section] / auth. Goodhart Charles // Inflation, Depression, and Economic Policy in the West / book auth. Courakis Anthony S.. - Totowa, New Jersey : Barnes and Noble Books, 1981.

[47] **The Tiger That Isn't: Seeing Through a World of Numbers** [Book] / auth. Blastland Michael and Dilnot Andrew. - [s.l.] : Profile Books, 2008.

[48] **Coronavirus: Why are international comparisons difficult?** [Online] / auth. Morris Chris and Reuben Anthony // BBC News. - June 17, 2020. - https://www.bbc.co.uk/news/52311014.

[49] **Mortality Analyses** [Online] / auth. John Hopkins University & Medicine // John Hopkins University & Medicine Coronavirus Resource Center. - 2022. - https://coronavirus.jhu.edu/data/mortality.

[50] **A-Levels 2021 Another Year of Grade Inflation?** [Online] / auth. Smithers Alan // The University of Buckingham. - August 2021. - https://www.buckingham.ac.uk/wp-content/uploads/2021/08/CoveredAL2021.pdf.

[51] **Fiddling the figures** [Online] / auth. Davies Nick // The Guardian. - July 11, 2003. - https://www.theguardian.com/uk/2003/jul/11/ukcrime.prisonsandprobation1.

[52] **Whistle blower muzzled after 'culture of manipulaton' alert** [Online] / auth. The Guardian // The Guardian. - 18 March 1999. - https://www.theguardian.com/uk/1999/mar/18/5.

[53] **Performance Management, Gaming and Police Practice** [Online] / auth. Patrick Rodger // University of Birmingham. - https://etheses.bham.ac.uk/id/eprint/534/1/Patrick09PhD.pdf.

[54] **Police officers manipulate the statistics to meet robbery and burglary targets** [Online] / auth. Foggo Daniel and Fellstorm Carl // The Telegraph. - 17 April 2005. - https://www.telegraph.co.uk/news/uknews/1487992/Police-officers-manipulate-the-statistics-to-meet-robbery-and-burglary-targets.html.

[55] **Watching the detectives: how the police cheat in fight against crime** [Online] / auth. The Guardian // The Guardian. - 18 March 1999. - https://www.theguardian.com/uk/1999/mar/18/6.

[56] **Oliver Schmidt jailed for seven years for Volkswagen emissions scam** [Online] / auth. Rushe Dominic // The Guardian. - 6 December 2017. - https://www.theguardian.com/business/2017/dec/06/oliver-schmidt-jailed-volkswagen-emissions-scam-seven-years.

[57] **Volkswagen emissions scandal** [Online] / auth. Wikipedia // Wikipedia. - https://en.wikipedia.org/wiki/Volkswagen_emissions_scandal.

[58] **Volkswagen: The scandal explained** [Online] / auth. Hotten Russell // BBC News. - 2015 December 2015. - https://www.bbc.co.uk/news/business-34324772.

[59] **Volkswagen says diesel scandal has cost it 31.3 billion euros** [Online] / auth. Reuters Staff // Reuters. - 17 March 2020. - https://www.reuters.com/article/us-volkswagen-results-diesel-idUSKBN2141JB.

[60] **Performance Watch: What will be the new P45 target?** [Online] / auth. Illman James // Health Service Journal. - 8 May 2019. - https://www.hsj.co.uk/expert-briefings/performance-watch-what-will-be-the-new-p45-target/7025016.article.

[61] **Gaming in Targetworld: The Targets Approach to Managing British Public Services** [Article] / auth. Hood Christopher // Public Administration Review. - July / August 2006. - pp. 515 - 521.

[62] **Perverse incentive** [Online] / auth. Wikipedia // Wikipedia. - https://en.wikipedia.org/wiki/Perverse_incentive#The_original_cobra_effect.

[63] **Great Hanoi Rat Massacre** [Online] / auth. Wikipedia // Wikipedia. - https://en.wikipedia.org/wiki/Great_Hanoi_Rat_Massacre.

[64] **Mapping disease: John Snow and Cholera** [Online] / auth. Begum Fahema // Royal College of Surgeons of England. - 09 December 2016. - https://www.rcseng.ac.uk/library-and-publications/library/blog/mapping-disease-john-snow-and-cholera/.

[65] **1854 Broad Street cholera outbreak** [Online] / auth. Wikipedia // Wikipedia. - https://en.wikipedia.org/wiki/1854_Broad_Street_cholera_outbreak.

[66] **On the mode of communication of cholera** [Book] / auth. Snow John. - London : John Churchill, 1855.

[67] **The OODA Loop and the Half-Beat** [Online] / auth. Luft Alastair // The Strategy Bridge. - 17 March 2020. - https://thestrategybridge.org/the-bridge/2020/3/17/the-ooda-loop-and-the-half-beat.

[68] **Why creationism is wrong and evolution is right** [Online] / auth. Jones Steve // YouTube. - https://www.youtube.com/watch?v=0ZlQybxkTGM&t=203s.

Professor Steve Jones explains what happened in his lecture on evolution. Matthew Syed later picked up the story in his book, *Black Box Thinking*.

[69] **Thinking in Systems: A Primer** [Book] / auth. Meadows Donella H.. - [s.l.] : Chelsea Green Publishing, 2008.

[70] **Outliers: The Story of Success** [Book] / auth. Gladwell Malcolm. - [s.l.] : Little, Brown and Company, 2008.

[71] **What does Trump actually believe on climate change?** [Online] / auth. Cheung Helier // BBC News. - 23 January 2020. - https://www.bbc.co.uk/news/world-us-canada-51213003.

[72] **Climate Change: Global Temperature** [Online] / auth. Lindsey Rebecca and Dahlman Luann // Climate.Gov. - 28 June 2022. - https://www.climate.gov/news-features/understanding-climate/climate-change-global-temperature.

[73] **Ripples from the Zambezi** [Book] / auth. Sirolli Ernesto. - [s.l.] : New Society Publishers, 1999.

As well as his book, Sirolli gives an excellent TED Talk.

[74] **The Toaster Project: Or a Heroic Attempt to Build a Simple Electric Appliance from Scratch** [Book] / auth. Thwaites Thomas. - [s.l.] : Princeton Architectural Press, 2011.

Leonard Read makes a similar point in his 1958 essay: *I, Pencil*

[75] **Weird Ideas that Work 11 1/2 Ways to Promote, Manage and Sustain Innovation** [Book] / auth. Sutton Robert I.. - [s.l.] : Allen Lane, 2002.

[76] **Sydney Opera House** [Online] / auth. Wikipedia // Wikipedia. - https://en.wikipedia.org/wiki/Sydney_Opera_House.

[77] **Planning Fallacy [Online]** / auth. Wikipedia // Wikipedia. - https://en.wikipedia.org/wiki/Planning_fallacy.

[78] **Abandoned NHS IT system has cost £10bn so far** [Online] / auth. Syal Rajeev // The Guardian. - 18 September 2013. - https://www.theguardian.com/society/2013/sep/18/nhs-records-system-10bn.

[79] **'No single reason' why Police Scotland i6 IT project failed, Audit Scotland concludes** [Online] / auth. Davidson Jenni // Holyrood. - 9 March 2017. - https://www.holyrood.com/news/view,no-single-reason-why-police-scotland-i6-it-project-failed-audit-scotland-concludes_13221.htm.

[80] **Delusions of Success: How Optimism Undermines Executives' Decisions** [Article] / auth. Lovallo Dan and Kahneman Daniel // Harvard Business Review Home. - July 2003.

[81] **Mumbai's Models of Service Excellence** [Article] / auth. Thomke Stefan // Harverd Business Review. - November 2012.

[82] **How dabbawalas became the world's best food delivery system** [Online] / auth. Henderson Emma // Independent. - 4 August 2017. - https://www.independent.co.uk/life-style/food-and-drink/dabbawalas-food-delivery-system-mumbai-india-lunchbox-work-lunch-tiffin-dabbas-a7859701.html.

[83] **Dabbawalas: Mumbai's lunchbox carriers** [Online] / auth. Pilling David and Chilkoti Avantika // Financial Times. - 31 July 2015. - https://www.ft.com/content/f3b3cbca-362c-11e5-b05b-b01debd57852.

[84] **Sweat the small stuff** [Online] / auth. Sutherland Rory // TED. - 2010. - https://www.ted.com/talks/rory_sutherland_sweat_the_small_stuff.

[85] **Fixing a toxic work culture: Breaking down barriers** [Online] / auth. Relihan Tom // MIT Management Sloan School. - 29 May 2019. - https://mitsloan.mit.edu/ideas-made-to-matter/fixing-a-toxic-work-culture-breaking-down-barriers.

[86] **Facing $17 billion loss, color-coding helped Alan Mulally turn around Ford** [Online] / auth. Muller David // Michigan Live. - 24 July 2016. - https://www.mlive.com/auto/2016/07/alan_mulally_ralph_nader_induc.html.

[87] **How Ford's Alan Mulally turned around its fortunes** [Online] / auth. Leggett Theo // BBC News. - 01 July 2014. - https://www.bbc.co.uk/news/business-28087325.

[88] **Meltdown** [Book] / auth. Clearfield Chris and Tilcsik Andras. - [s.l.] : Penguin, 2018.

[89] **June 2009 Washington Metro train collision** [Online] / auth. Wikipedia // Wikipedia. - https://en.wikipedia.org/wiki/June_2009_Washington_Metro_train_collision.

[90] **Collision of Two Washington Metropolitan Area Transit Authority Metrorail Trains Near Fort Totten Station Washington, DC** [Online] / auth. National Transportation Safety Board // National Transportation Safety Board. - 27 July 2010. - https://www.ntsb.gov/investigations/AccidentReports/Reports/RAR1002.pdf.

[91] **US Airways Flight1549** [Online] / auth. Wikipedia // Wikipedia. - https://en.wikipedia.org/wiki/US_Airways_Flight_1549.

[92] **Black Box Thinking** [Book] / auth. Syed Matthew. - [s.l.] : Penguin, 2015.

[93] **Systems Thinking Speech** [Online] / auth. Ackoff Russell L. // You Tube. - 1994. - https://www.youtube.com/watch?v=EbLh7rZ3rhU.

[94] **'Moonlight' or 'La La Land'? Best Picture Mix-up at Oscars** [Online] / auth. Eyewitness News // YouTube. - 26 February 2017. - https://www.youtube.com/watch?v=8KeOxeuiZjs.

[95] **Warren Beatty Explains the Big Oscars Mix Up** [Online] / auth. The Graham Norton Show // YouTube. - 14 April 2017. - https://www.youtube.com/watch?v=NRT5jTrnJPM.

[96] **Oscars envelope handler responsible for Best Picture mix-up was 'too busy tweeting' to do their job properly** [Online] / auth. Hooton Christopher // Independent. - 28 February 2017. - https://www.independent.co.uk/arts-entertainment/films/news/brian-cullinan-twitter-oscars-2017-best-picture-film-mixup-la-la-land-moonlight-pwc-tweeting-envelope-responsible-a7603176.html.

[97] **Why Typography Matters — Especially At The Oscars** [Online] / auth. Bannister Benjamin // Medium. - 27 February 2017. - https://medium.com/free-code-camp/why-typography-matters-especially-at-the-oscars-f7b00e202f22.

[98] **One big change to this year's Oscars could have played a part in the best picture envelope mishap** [Online] / auth. Acuna Kirsten // Insider. - 28 February 2017. - https://www.insider.com/oscars-changed-this-years-envelopes-2017-2017-2.

[99] **Meet the two PwC partners who handed out the Oscar envelopes** [Online] / auth. Burke Tim // Market Watch. - 27 February 2017. - https://www.marketwatch.com/story/meet-the-two-people-who-already-know-the-oscar-winners-2017-02-24.

[100] **The Oscars Have an Intense, Six-Step Plan to Avoid Another Envelope Disaster** [Online] / auth. Robinson Joanna // Vanity Fair. - 22 January 2018. - https://www.vanityfair.com/hollywood/2018/01/oscars-envelope-new-rules-moonlight-la-la-land.

[101] **6 new rules to prevent Oscars envelope gaffe** [Online] / auth. Cohen Sandy // WHSV. - 2018 January 2018. - https://www.whsv.com/content/news/6-new-rules-to-prevent-Oscars-envelope-gaffe-470579583.html.

[102] **Eighth Air Force** [Online] / auth. Wikipedia // Wikipedia. - https://en.wikipedia.org/wiki/Eighth_Air_Force.

[103] **Life And Death In Bomber Command** [Online] / auth. Imperial War Museum // Imperial War Museum. - https://www.iwm.org.uk/history/life-and-death-in-bomber-command.

[104] **The Human Factor** [Book] / auth. Vicente Kim. - [s.l.] : Random House, 2004.

[105] **Robotic Surgery** [Online] / auth. The Leeds Teaching Hospitals // The Leeds Teaching Hospitals NHS Trust. - https://www.leedsth.nhs.uk/a-z-of-services/urology/procedures/robotic-surgery/.

[106] **The Evidence Behind Robot-Assisted Abdominopelvic Surgery** [Journal] / auth. Dhanani Nalia H. [et al.] // Annals of Internal Medicine. - 2021. - pp. 1110-1117.

[107] **The Checklist Manifesto** [Book] / auth. Gawande Atul. - [s.l.] : Metropolitan Books, 2009.

[108] **A Surgical Safety Checklist to Reduce Morbidity and Mortality in a Global Population** [Journal] / auth. Alex B. Haynes Thomas G. Weiser, // The New England Journal of Medicine. - 2009. - pp. 491-499.

[109] **Crazy from the Heat** [Book] / auth. Roth David Lee. - [s.l.] : Hyperion, 1997.

[110] **Excuse me, there's a fly in my…** [Online] / auth. The Design Psych // Medium. - 12 January 2011. - https://medium.com/designerpsychology/excuse-me-theres-a-fly-in-my-ecc10fb176da.

[111] **The coal gas story. United Kingdom suicide rates, 1960-71** [Journal] / auth. Kreitman Norman // British Journal of Preventative & Social Medicine. - 1976. - pp. 30, 86-93.

[112] **Improved Safety Through Improved Technical Measures?** [Book Section] / auth. Aschenbrenner K. M. and Biehl B. // Challenges to Accident Prevention The Issue of Risk Compensation Behaviour / book auth. Rüdiger Trimpop Gerald J. S. Wilde. - Groningen : Styx Publications, 1994.

[113] **Reducing bicycle accidents: a re-evaluation of the impacts of the CPSC bicycle standard and helmet use** [Journal] / auth. Rogers G. B. // Journal of Products Liability. - 1988. - pp. 11:307-317.

[114] **Adult smoking habits in the UK**: 2019 [Online] / auth. Windsor-Shellard Ben [et al.] // Office for National Statistics. - 7 July 2020. - https://www.ons.gov.uk/peoplepopulationandcommunity/healthandsocialcare/healthandlifeexpectancies/bulletins/adultsmokinghabitsingreatbritain/2019#data-on-smokers-who-have-quit-and-smokers-who-intend-to-quit-great-britain-1974-to-2019.

[115] **Georgia investigation into cheating in Atlanta Public Schools** [Online] / auth. Wilson Robert E., Bowers Michael J. and Hyde Richard L. // Internet Archive. - 06 July 2011. - https://archive.org/details/215260-georgia-investigation/.

[116] **Georgia cheating scandal: 11 teachers found guilty of racketeering** [Online] / auth. Kasperkevic Jana // The Guardian. - 1 April 2015. - https://www.theguardian.com/us-news/2015/apr/01/atlanta-teachers-found-guilty-cheating.

[117] **Trial begins for Atlanta teachers accused of inflating test scores** [Online] / auth. Jarvie Jenny // Los Angeles Times. - 29 September 2014. - https://www.latimes.com/nation/la-na-atlanta-schools-cheating-trial-20140929-story.html.

[118] **Are drastic swings in CRCT scores valid?** [Online] / auth. Vogel Heather and Perry John // Atlanta Journal-Constitution. - 2009. - http://www.ajc.com/news/local/are-drastic-swings-crct-scores-valid/1uNxbbiLUZjvYQx6gMkyyN/.

[119] **Wrong Answer** [Online] / auth. Aviv Rachel // The New Yorker. - 14 July 2014. - https://www.newyorker.com/magazine/2014/07/21/wrong-answer.

[120] **No Child Left Behind Act** [Online] / auth. Wikipedia // Wikipedia. - https://en.wikipedia.org/wiki/No_Child_Left_Behind_Act.

[121] **Beverly Hall dies; criminal case — and her legacy — unresolved** [Online] / auth. Judd Alan // The Atlanta Journal-Constitution. - 2 March 2015. - https://www.ajc.com/news/breaking-news/beverly-hall-dies-criminal-case-and-her-legacy-unresolved/kWdRFDoS3Cze42IQTfYJOK/.

[122] **GAO: 40 states have suspected cheating on K-12 tests** [Online] / auth. Layton Lyndsey // The Washington Post. - 17 May 2013. - https://www.washingtonpost.com/local/education/gao-40-states-have-suspected-cheating-on-k-12-tests/2013/05/17/a366542c-bf1d-11e2-97d4-a479289a31f9_story.html.

[123] **Schools 'bribing pupils' to cheat Ofsted inspections** [Online] / auth. Paton Graeme // The Telegraph. - 06 January 2012. - https://www.telegraph.co.uk/education/educationnews/8995377/Schools-bribing-pupils-to-cheat-Ofsted-inspections.html.

[124] **Anger as fatal jab doctor freed** [Online] / auth. BBC News // BBC News. - 23 September 2003. - http://news.bbc.co.uk/1/hi/health/3133076.stm.

[125] **External Inquiry into the adverse incident that occurred at Queen's Medical Centre, Nottingham, 4th January 2001** [Report] / auth. Toft Professor Brian. - [s.l.] : Department of Health, 2001.

[126] **Avoiding the avoidable to improve the safety of NHS care** [Online] / auth. Donaldson Liam // Parliamentary And Health Service Ombudsman. - December 2018. - https://www.ombudsman.org.uk/news-and-blog/podcast/transcript-radio-ombudsman-9-avoiding-avoidable-improve-safety-nhs-care.

[127] **Memorandum by Professor Brian Toft (PS 83)** [Online] / auth. Toft Professor Brian // Parliament - Patient Safety - Health Committee. - November 2008. - https://publications.parliament.uk/pa/cm200809/cmselect/cmhealth/151/151we26.htm.

[128] **Sydney hospital blunder exposed** [Online] / auth. ABC News // ABC News. - 5 May 2004. - https://www.abc.net.au/news/2004-05-06/sydney-hospital-blunder-exposed/1971302.

[129] **Patient Safety Alert Stage Three: Directive Non-Luer spinal (intrathecal) devices for chemotherapy** [Online] / auth. NHS England // NHS England. - February 20, 2014. - https://www.england.nhs.uk/wp-content/uploads/2019/12/non-Luer-spinal-supp.pdf.

[130] **Teenager given wrong drug dies** [Online] / auth. Dyer Clare // The Guardian. - 2001 February 2001. - https://www.theguardian.com/society/2001/feb/03/health.uknews.

[131] **Data on speciality treatments** [Online] / auth. NHS // My NHS. - https://www.nhs.uk/mynhs/specialties.html.

[132] **The Human Side of Enterprise** [Book] / auth. McGregor Douglas. - [s.l.] : McGraw-Hill, 1960.

[133] **Pygmalion in Management** [Online] / auth. Livingston J. Sterling // Harvard Business Review. - January 2003. - https://hbr.org/2003/01/pygmalion-in-management.

[134] **The effect of experimenter bias on the performance of the albino rat** [Journal] / auth. Rosenthal Robert A. and Fode K. L. // Behavioral Science. - 1963. - pp. 8, 183-189.

[135] **Pygmalion in the Classroom** [Journal] / auth. Rosenthal Robert A. and Jacobson Lenore // The Urban Review. - 1968. - pp. 3, 16-20.

[136] **Pygmalion goes to boot camp: Expectancy, leadership, and trainee performance** [Journal] / auth. Eden D. and Shani Abraham. B. // Journal of Applied Psychology. - 1982. - pp. 67(2), 194–199.

[137] **Interpersonal Expectancy Effects: A 30-Year Perspective** [Journal] / auth. Rosenthal Robert // Current Directions in Psychological Science. - [s.l.] : Cambridge University Press, December 1994. - 6 : Vol. 3. - pp. 176-179.

[138] **Drive, The Surprising Truth About What Motivated Us** [Book] / auth. Pink Daniel H.. - New York : Riverhead Books, 2009.

[139] **The Influence Of Strength Of Drive on Functional Fixedness and Perceptual** [Article] / auth. Glucksberg Sam // Journal of Experimentsl Psychology. - [s.l.] : American Psychological Association, January 1962. - 1 : Vol. 63. - pp. 36-41.

[140] **Undermining Children's Intrinsic Interest with Extrinsic Reward: A Test of the Overjustification Effect** [Article] / auth. Lepper Mark R, Greene David and Nisbett Richard E // Journal of Personality and Social Psychology. - [s.l.] : American Psychological Association, 1973. - Vol. 28. - pp. 129-137.

[141] **Moral behaviour in animals** [Online] / auth. Waal Frans de // TED. - April 2012. - https://www.ted.com/talks/frans_de_waal_moral_behavior_in_animals.

[142] **The New Science of Building Great Teams** [Online] / auth. Pentland Alex // Harvard Business Review. - April 2012. - https://hbr.org/2012/04/the-new-science-of-building-great-teams.

[143] **Why More and More Companies Are Ditching Performance Ratings** [Online] / auth. Rock David and Jones Beth // Harvard Business Review. - 8 September 2015. - https://hbr.org/2015/09/why-more-and-more-companies-are-ditching-performance-ratings.

[144] **Overcoming dysfunctional momentum: Organizational safety as a social achievement** [Journal] / auth. Barton Michelle A. and Sutcliffe Kathleen M. // Human Relations. - 2009. - pp. 1327-1356.

[145] **TWA Flight 514** [Online] / auth. Wikipedia // Wikipedia. - https://en.wikipedia.org/wiki/TWA_Flight_514.

[146] **Industrial Accident Prevention: A Scientific Approach** [Book] / auth. Heinrich Herbert William. - [s.l.] : McGraw-Hill book Company, Incorporated, 1931.

[147] **Program Briefing** [Online] / auth. Aviation Safety Reporting System // Aviation Safety Reporting System. - https://asrs.arc.nasa.gov/overview/summary.html.

[148] **40 Years of Safer Aviation Through Reporting** [Online] / auth. Colen Jerry // NASA. - 2018 September 2016. - https://www.nasa.gov/ames/feature/40-Years-of-Safer-Aviation-through-Reporting.

[149] **IT WAS PILOT ERROR' First pictures of Russian plane crash pilot who the Kremlin 'blames' for deadly air disaster as search teams pull Tu-154 fuselage from Black Sea** [Online] / auth. Stewart Will // The Sun. - 2016 December 2016. - https://www.thesun.co.uk/news/2479358/russian-plane-crash-pilot-pictures-tu-154-jet-russia-black-sea/.

[150] **Russian Defence Ministry Tupolev Tu-154 crash** [Online] / auth. Wikipedia // Wikipedia. - https://en.wikipedia.org/wiki/2016_Russian_Defence_Ministry_Tupolev_Tu-154_crash.

[151] **1997 Letter to Shareholders** [Online] / auth. Bezos, Jeffrey P. // About Amazon. - December 1997. - https://s2.q4cdn.com/299287126/files/doc_financials/annual/Shareholderletter97.pdf.

[152] **Four Peaks: My interview with Jeff Bezos** [Online] / auth. HRH Media // YouTube. - 14 September 2013. - https://youtu.be/vhDRBPCOxmA?t=429.

[153] **In conversation with Jeff Bezos: CEO of the internet** [Online] / auth. Levy Steven // Wired. - 12 12 2011. - https://www.wired.co.uk/article/ceo-of-the-internet.

[154] **2003 Letter to Shareholders** [Online] / auth. Bezos, Jeffrey P. // All About Amazon. - December 2003. - https://s2.q4cdn.com/299287126/files/doc_financials/annual/2003_-Shareholder_-Letter041304.pdf.

[155] **The long and short of the quarterly reports controversy** [Online] / auth. Walker Owen // Financial Times. - 02 July 2018. - https://www.ft.com/content/e61046bc-7a2e-11e8-8e67-1e1a0846c475.

[156] **To the Shareholders of Berkshire Hathaway Inc.:** [Online] / auth. Buffett Warren E // Berkshire Hathaway Inc.. - 23 February 2019. - https://www.berkshirehathaway.com/letters/2018ltr.pdf.

[157] **Smallpox** [Online] / auth. Wikipedia // Wikipedia. - https://en.wikipedia.org/wiki/Smallpox.

[158] **The Smallpox Story: Life and Death of an Old Disease** [Article] / auth. Behbehani Abbas M // Microbiological Reviews. - [s.l.] : American Society for Microbiology, December 1983. - 4 : Vol. 47. - pp. 455-509.

[159] **Smallpox eradication-the final battle'** [Journal] / auth. Henderson D. A. // Journal of Clinical Pathology. - 1975. - pp. 28, 843-849.

[160] **Polio eradication** [Online] / auth. Wikipedia // Wikipedia. - https://en.wikipedia.org/wiki/Polio_eradication.

[161] **CIA organised fake vaccination drive to get Osama bin Laden's family DNA** [Online] / auth. Shah Saeed // The Guardian. - 11 July 2011. - https://www.theguardian.com/world/2011/jul/11/cia-fake-vaccinations-osama-bin-ladens-dna.

[162] **Microsoft** [Online] / auth. Wikipedia // Wikipedia. - https://en.wikipedia.org/wiki/Microsoft.

[163] **Microsoft's Lost Decade** [Online] / auth. Eichenwald Kurk // Vanity Fair. - 24 July 2012. - https://www.vanityfair.com/news/business/2012/08/microsoft-lost-mojo-steve-ballmer.

[164] **Vitality curve** [Online] / auth. Wikipedia // Wikipedia. - https://en.wikipedia.org/wiki/Vitality_curve.

[165] **Ballmer memo: Microsoft plans unprecedented boost in employee compensation, simpler reviews** [Online] / auth. Bishop Todd // Geek Wire. - 21 April 2011. - https://www.geekwire.com/2011/ballmer-memo-microsoft-plans-unprecedented-boost-employee-compensation/.

[166] **Stack Rank This!** [Book] / auth. 154160 and 191855. - [s.l.] : CreateSpace Independent Publishing Platform, 2012.

[167] **Microsoft chucks controversial staff-ranking system** [Online] / auth. Foley Mary Jo // CNET. - 12 Nov 2013. - https://www.cnet.com/tech/tech-industry/microsoft-chucks-controversial-staff-ranking-system/.

[168] **How Microsoft made the stunning transformation from Evil Empire to Cool Kid** [Online] / auth. Wadhwa Vivek, Amala Ismail and Salkever Alex // Fortune. - 21 December 2021. - https://fortune.com/2021/12/21/microsoft-cultural-transformation-book-excerpt-satya-nadella/.

[169] **The $1 trillion miracle of Microsoft** [Online] / auth. Carr Austin and Bass Dina // Australian Financial Review. - 10 May 2019. - https://www.afr.com/technology/the-1-trillion-miracle-of-microsoft-20190507-p51kr7.

[170] **Hit Refresh: The Quest to Rediscover Microsoft's Soul and Imagine a Better Future for Everyone** [Book] / auth. Nadella Satya, Shaw Greg and Tracie Nichols Jill. - [s.l.] : Harper Collins, 2017.

[171] **Dover delays: Coaches full of children stuck for 12 HOURS as thousands in Easter getaway** [Online] / auth. Weston Katie // Mirror. - 1 April 2023. - https://www.mirror.co.uk/news/uk-news/dover-delays-coaches-full-children-29604571.

[172] **School coaches face 12-hour waits at Dover amid Easter travel chaos** [Online] / auth. Corless Blathnaid // The Telegraph. - 1 04 2023. - https://www.telegraph.co.uk/news/2023/04/01/dover-chaos-school-coaches-delays-easter-getaway/.

[173] **@Sillytees** [Online] / auth. Bealing Mike // Twitter. - s April 2023. - https://twitter.com/Sillytees/status/1642802655805276163.

[174] **Suella Braverman denies Brexit to blame for Dover queues of 14 hours** [Online] / auth. Crerar Pippa and Vinter Robyn // The Guardian. - 2 April 2023. - https://www.theguardian.com/politics/2023/apr/02/suella-braverman-denies-brexit-to-blame-for-dover-queues-of-14-hours.

[175] **UK Travellers face third day of holiday disruption at Dover** [Online] / auth. Cameron-Chileshe Jasmine // Financial Times. - 2 April 2023. - https://www.ft.com/content/a8acb595-8203-4a2e-83c2-454a00d374c3.

[176] **The GE Work-Out How to Implement GE's Revolutionary Method for Busting Bureaucracy & Attacking Organizational Problems - Fast** [Book] / auth. Ulrich David, Kerr Steve and Ashkenas Ron. - [s.l.] : McGraw-Hill Education, 2002.

Work-Out is great. Developed by General Electric under Jack Welch, it is redemption for their popularisation of the Vitality Curve.

[177] Net Promoter Scores (NPS) can be between -100 and + 100. An online search will tell you how to survey customers (or employees) and calculate the result. The number by itself isn't a diagnostic tool, but repeated surveying will show if you are getting better.

Index

Thrive

/'θraɪʊ/'

thrived or throve; thrived also thriven; thriving

intransitive verb

to grow vigorously:

to gain wealth or possessions:

to progress towards a goal despite or because of circumstances:

> *His business thrived in the years before the war.*

> *She seems to thrive on praise.*

synonyms

burgeon (literary), prosper, flourish, triumph